the
Unofficial
Guide® to
Walt Disney
World
with Kids
1st Edition

the Unofficial Guide® to Walt Disney World with Kids

1st Edition

Bob Sehlinger

Macmillan • USA

Every effort has been made to ensure the accuracy of information throughout this book. Bear in mind, however, that prices, schedules, etc., are constantly changing. Readers should always verify information before making final plans.

Macmillan Travel
Macmillan General Reference USA, Inc.
1633 Broadway
New York, New York 10019-6785

Produced by Menasha Ridge Press

ISBN 0-02-863352-0
ISSN 1523-0627

Manufactured in the United States of America
10 9 8 7 6 5 4 3 2 1
First edition

Contents

List of Maps

Acknowledgments

Special thanks to our field research team who rendered a Herculean effort in what must have seemed like a fantasy version of Sartre's *No Exit* to the tune of "It's a Small World." We hope you all recover to tour another day.

Betsy Amster	Amber Morris
Lynne Bachleda	Madeline O'Bryan
Molly Burns	Taylor O'Bryan (the Human Probe)
Holly Cross	Tiffany Prewitt-McClain
Leslie Cummins	Rebecca Self
Shelley DeLuca	Grace Walton
Chris Mohney	Barbara Williams

Peals of laughter and much appreciation to nationally renowned cartoonists Tami Knight and William Nealy for their brilliant and insightful work.

Psychologists Dr. Karen Turnbow, Dr. Gayle Janzen, and Dr. Joan Burns provided much insight concerning the experiences of young children at Walt Disney World. "Hotel Women" Holly Cross and Tiffany Prewitt-McClain inspected many dozens of hotels. *Unofficial Guide to Cruises* author Kay Showker assisted with our coverage of the Disney Cruise Line.

Many thanks also to Holly Cross, Molly Harrison, Laura Poole, and Jude Grant, for production and editorial work on this book. Caroline Carr, Steve Jones, and Amy Sloan earned our appreciation for their fine work and for keeping tight deadlines in providing the typography. Cartography was provided by Brian Taylor and Steve Jones, and the index was prepared by Sylvia Coates.

Introduction

How Come "Unofficial"?
DECLARATION OF INDEPENDENCE

The author and researchers of this guide specifically and categorically declare that they are and always have been totally independent of the Walt Disney Company, Inc.; of Disneyland, Inc.; of Walt Disney World, Inc.; and of any and all other members of the Disney corporate family not listed.

The authors believe in the wondrous variety, joy, and excitement of the Walt Disney World attractions. At the same time, we recognize that Walt Disney World is a business, with the same profit motivations as businesses the world over. In this guide we represent and serve you, the consumer. If a restaurant serves bad food, or a gift item is overpriced, or a certain ride isn't worth the wait, we can say so, and in the process we hope to make your visit more fun, efficient, and economical.

WHY SO MANY BOOKS?

We've been writing about Walt Disney World for almost 20 years. When we started, Walt Disney World pretty much consisted of just the Magic Kingdom theme park and a few hotels. Since then, Walt Disney World has grown to the size of a city and is equally if not more complex. Our comprehensive *Unofficial Guide to Walt Disney World,* tipping the scales at almost 800 pages, still provides the most in-depth and objective coverage of any Walt Disney World guide and is our basic reference work on the subject.

As thorough as we try to make *The Unofficial Guide to Walt Disney World,* there is not sufficient space to share all of the tips

and information that may be important and useful to some of our readers. Thus, we have developed four additional Walt Disney World guides, all designed to work in conjunction with what we call "the big book." Each of the four, including this guide for families with children, provides specialized information tailored to very specific Walt Disney World visitors. Although some tips from the big book (like arriving at the theme parks early) are echoed or elaborated herein, most of the information is unique and was developed especially for *The Unofficial Guide to Walt Disney World with Kids.* Just as there's not space in the big book for the family-oriented material presented here; likewise, we can't cram all of the detailed information from *The Unofficial Guide to Walt Disney World* into this guide. Rather, the two guides are designed to work together and complement each other.

In addition to *The Unofficial Guide to Walt Disney World,* also by Bob Sehlinger (784 pages; $16.95), the following titles are available:

Mini-Mickey: The Pocket-Sized Unofficial Guide to Walt Disney World, by Bob Sehlinger; 320 pages; $10.95

Inside Disney: The Incredible Story of Walt Disney World and the Man Behind the Mouse, by Eve Zibart; 240 pages; $9.95

The Unofficial Guide to Walt Disney World for Grown-Ups, by Eve Zibart; 192 pages; $9.95

Beyond Disney: The Unofficial Guide to Universal Florida, Sea World, and the Best of Central Florida, by Bob Sehlinger and Amber Morris; 192 pages; $9.95

Mini-Mickey is a nice, portable, *Cliff Notes* version of *The Unofficial Guide to Walt Disney World.* Updated annually, it distills information from this comprehensive guide to help short-stay or last-minute visitors quickly decide how to plan their limited hours at Walt Disney World. *Inside Disney* is a behind-the-scenes unauthorized history of Walt Disney World, and it is loaded with all the amazing facts and great stories that we can't squeeze into the big book. *The Unofficial Guide to Walt Disney World for Grown-Ups* helps adults traveling without children make the most of their Disney vacation, and *Beyond Disney* is a complete consumer guide to the non-Disney attractions, restaurants, outdoor recreation, and nightlife in Orlando and central Florida. All of the guides are available from Macmillan Travel and at most bookstores.

THE MUSIC OF LIFE

Although it is common in our culture to see life as a journey from cradle to grave, Alan Watts, a noted late-twentieth-century philosopher, saw it somewhat differently: He viewed life not as a journey but as a dance. In a journey, he said, you are trying to get somewhere, and are consequently always looking ahead, anticipating the way stations, and thinking about the end. Although a journey is a popular metaphor for life, particularly in the West, it is generally characterized by a driven, goal-oriented mentality, a way of living and being that often inhibits those who subscribe to the metaphor from being in the present and savoring each moment of life.

When you dance, by contrast, you hear the music and move in harmony with the rhythm. Like life, a dance has a beginning and an end. But unlike life, your objective is not to get to the end, but to enjoy the dance while the music plays. You are totally in the moment and care nothing about where on the floor you stop when the dance is done.

As you begin to contemplate your Walt Disney World vacation, you may not have much patience for a philosophical discussion about journeys and dancing. But, you see, it *is* relevant. If you are like most travel guide readers, you are apt to plan and organize, to anticipate and control, and you like things to go smoothly. And, truth be told, this leads us to suspect that you are a person that looks ahead and is outcome oriented. You may even feel a bit of pressure concerning your vacation. Vacations, after all, are special events and expensive ones as well. So you work hard to make the most of your vacation.

We also believe that work and planning and organization are important, and at Walt Disney World they are even essential. But if they become your focus, you won't be able to hear the music and enjoy the dance. Though a lot of dancing these days resembles highly individualized *grand mal* seizures, there was a time when each dance involved specific steps, which you committed to memory. At first you were tentative and awkward, but eventually the steps became second nature and you didn't have to think about them anymore.

Metaphorically, this is what we want for you and your children or grandchildren as you embark on your Walt Disney World vacation. We want you to learn the steps ahead of time, so that when you're on your vacation and the music plays, you will be able to hear it, and you and your children will dance with grace and ease.

Your Personal Trainers

We're your Walt Disney World personal trainers. We will help you plan and enjoy your Walt Disney World vacation. Together we will make sure that it really *is* a vacation, as opposed to say, an ordeal or an expensive way to experience heat stroke. Our objective, simply put, is to ensure that you and your children have fun.

Because this book is specifically for adults traveling with children, we'll concentrate on your special needs and challenges. We'll share our most useful tips as well as the travel secrets of more than 18,000 families interviewed over the 8 years we've covered Walt Disney World. For a more detailed, comprehensive coverage of Walt Disney World itself, pick up a copy of *The Unofficial Guide to Walt Disney World.*

Yes, You Can Do It

We'll start by saying that both enjoying and surviving a Walt Disney World vacation are possible. Millions of parents and grandparents have done it, and so can you. We do not, however, advise winging it. Your best shot at having a really great vacation comes from fully understanding the unique challenges of touring Walt Disney World with children.

About This Guide

Walt Disney World has been our beat for almost two decades, and we know it inside out. During those years we have observed many thousands of parents and grandparents trying—some successfully, others less so—to have a good time at Walt Disney World. Some of these, owing to unfortunate dynamics within the family, were doomed right from the start. Others were simply overwhelmed by the size and complexity of Walt Disney World, whereas still others fell victim to a lack of foresight, planning, and organization.

Walt Disney World is a better destination for some families than for others. Likewise, some families are more compatible on vacation than others. The likelihood of experiencing a truly wonderful Walt Disney World vacation transcends the theme parks and attractions offered. In fact, the theme parks and attractions are the only constants in the equation. The variables that will define the experience and determine its success or failure are intrinsic to your family, things like attitude, sense of humor, cohesiveness, stamina, flexibility, and conflict resolution.

The simple truth is that Walt Disney World will test you as a family. It will overwhelm you with choices and force you to make decisions about how to spend your time and money. It will wear you down physically as you cover mile after mile on foot and wait in endless lines touring the theme parks. You will have to respond to surprises (both good and bad), deal with hyper-stimulation as well as disappointment, and be able to reconcile your actual experience with sometimes unrealistic expectations.

This guide will forewarn and forearm you. It will help you decide whether a Walt Disney World vacation is good idea for you and your family at this particular time. It will help you sort out and address the attitudes and family dynamics that can ruin your good time. Most important, it will provide the confidence that comes with thorough self-examination coupled with good planning and realistic expectations.

LETTERS AND COMMENTS FROM READERS

Many of those who use *The Unofficial Guide to Walt Disney World* write us to make comments or share their own strategies for visiting Walt Disney World. We appreciate all such input, both positive and critical, and encourage our readers to continue writing. Readers' comments and observations are frequently incorporated into revised editions of the *Unofficial Guide* and have contributed immeasurably to its improvement. If you write us, you can rest assured that we won't release your name and address to any mailing list companies, direct mail advertisers, or any other third party.

How to Write the Author

Bob Sehlinger
The Unofficial Guide to Walt Disney World with Kids
P.O. Box 43673
Birmingham, AL 35243

When you write, put your address on both your letter and the envelope, since sometimes the two get separated. It is also a good idea to include your phone number. And remember, as travel writers, we're often out of the office for long periods of time, so forgive us if our response time is slow.

A Quick Tour of a Big World

Walt Disney World encompasses 43 square miles, an area twice as large as Manhattan island and roughly the same size as Boston. Situated strategically in this vast expanse are the Magic Kingdom, Epcot, Disney-MGM Studios, and the Animal Kingdom theme parks; three water parks; a botanical and zoological park; two nighttime entertainment areas; a sports complex; several golf courses, hotels, and campgrounds; almost 100 restaurants; four large, interconnected lakes; a shopping complex; three convention venues; a nature preserve; and a complete transportation system consisting of four-lane highways, elevated monorails, and a system of canals.

THE MAJOR THEME PARKS

The Magic Kingdom

When people think of Walt Disney World, most think of the Magic Kingdom. It comprises the collection of adventures, rides, shows symbolizing the Disney cartoon characters, and Cinderella Castle. Although the Magic Kingdom is only one element of Disney World, it remains its heart. The Magic Kingdom is divided into seven subareas or "lands," six of which are arranged around a central hub. First encountered is Main Street, U.S.A., which connects the Magic Kingdom entrance with the central hub. Clockwise around the hub are Adventureland, Frontierland, Liberty Square, Fantasyland, and Tomorrowland. Mickey's Toontown Fair, the first new land in the

Magic Kingdom since the park opened (originally named Mickey's Birthdayland), is situated along the Walt Disney Railroad on three acres between Fantasyland and Tomorrowland. Access is through Fantasyland or Tomorrowland or via the railroad. Three hotels (the Contemporary, Polynesian, and Grand Floridian Beach resorts) are close to the Magic Kingdom and are directly connected to it by monorail and boat. Two additional hotels, Shades of Green (formerly the Disney Inn) and Disney's Wilderness Lodge Resort, are nearby but aren't served by the monorail.

Epcot

Epcot opened in October 1982. Divided into two major areas, Future World and World Showcase, the park is twice as big as the Magic Kingdom and comparable in scope. Future World consists of futuristic pavilions relating to different themes concerning humankind's creativity and technological advancement. World Showcase, arranged around a 41-acre lagoon, presents the architectural, social, and cultural heritages of almost a dozen nations, with each country represented by replicas of famous landmarks and local settings familiar to world travelers. Epcot is more educationally oriented than the Magic Kingdom and has been repeatedly characterized as a sort of permanent World's Fair.

The five Epcot resort hotels—Disney's Beach Club, Disney's Yacht Club, Disney's BoardWalk Resort, the Walt Disney World Swan and the Walt Disney World Dolphin—are within a 5- to 15-minute walk of Epcot's "back door," International Gateway entrance. The hotels are also linked to the park by canal. Epcot is connected to the Magic Kingdom and its resort hotels by monorail.

Disney-MGM Studios

This 100-acre theme park opened in 1989 and is divided into two areas. The first is a theme park focusing on the past, present, and future of the motion picture and television industries. This section contains movie-theme rides and shows and covers about half of the Disney-MGM complex. Highlights include a re-creation of Hollywood and Sunset Boulevards from Hollywood's Golden Age, audience-participation shows on TV production

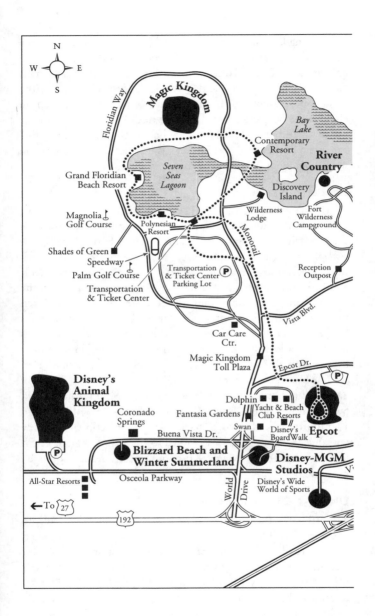

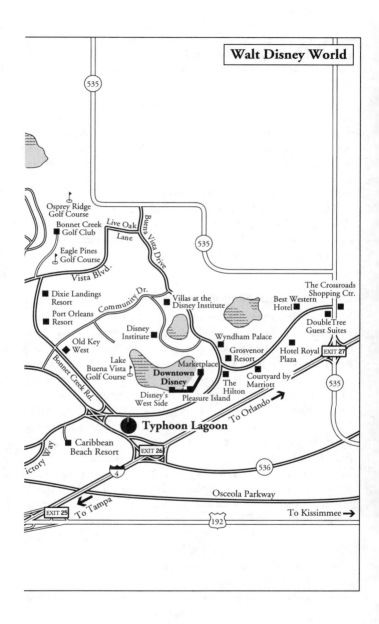

Walt Disney World

Osprey Ridge Golf Course
Bonnet Creek Golf Club
Eagle Pines Golf Course
Live Oak Lane
Buena Vista Drive
535
Vista Blvd.
Dixie Landings Resort
Community Dr.
Villas at the Disney Institute
The Crossroads Shopping Ctr.
Best Western Hotel
Port Orleans Resort
DoubleTree Guest Suites
Disney Institute
Wyndham Palace
Old Key West
Hotel Royal Plaza
EXIT 27
Lake Buena Vista Golf Course
Grosvenor Resort
Marketplace
Downtown Disney
Bonnet Creek Rd.
Courtyard by Marriott
535
Disney's West Side
The Hilton
Pleasure Island
To Orlando →
Typhoon Lagoon
Caribbean Beach Resort
Victory Way
EXIT 26
I-4
536
Osceola Parkway
EXIT 25
← To Tampa
192
To Kissimmee →

11

and sound effects, movie stunt demonstrations, a children's play area, and four high-tech rides: *The Twilight Zone* Tower of Terror, Star Tours, the Rock 'n' Roller Coaster, and The Great Movie Ride.

The second area is a working motion picture and television production facility encompassing three soundstages, a backlot of streets and sets, and creative support services. Public access is limited to studio tours, which take visitors behind the scenes for crash courses on Disney animation and movie making, including (on occasion) the opportunity to witness the actual shooting of a feature film, television show, or commercial.

Disney-MGM Studios is connected to other Walt Disney World areas by highway and canal, but not by monorail. Guests can park in the Studios' pay parking lot or commute by bus. Patrons staying in Epcot resort hotels can also reach the Studios by boat.

Disney's Animal Kingdom

More than five times the size of the Magic Kingdom, the Animal Kingdom combines zoological exhibits with rides, shows, and live entertainment. The park is arranged somewhat like the Magic Kingdom, in a hub-and-spoke configuration. A lush tropical rain forest called The Oasis serves as Main Street, funneling visitors to Safari Village at the center of the park. Dominated by the park's central icon, the 14-story-tall, hand-carved Tree of Life, Safari Village is the park's center, with services, shopping, and dining. From Safari Village, guests can access the theme areas: Africa, Asia, DinoLand U.S.A., Camp Minnie-Mickey, and the Beastly Kingdom (tentative name). Scheduled to open in phases, Safari Village, Africa, Camp Minnie-Mickey, and DinoLand U.S.A. came on-line in 1998, followed by Asia in 1999, with the Beastly Kingdom slated for 2001. Africa, the largest theme area at 100 acres, features free-roaming herds in a re-creation of the Serengeti Plain. Guests tour in open-air safari vehicles.

Disney's Animal Kingdom has its own pay parking lot and is connected to other Disney World destinations by the Disney bus system. Although for the moment, there are no hotels at the Animal Kingdom, the All-Star and Coronado Springs resorts are nearby.

THE WATER THEME PARKS

There are three major swimming theme parks in Walt Disney World: Typhoon Lagoon, River Country, and Blizzard Beach. Typhoon Lagoon is distinguished by a wave pool capable of making six-foot waves. River Country, a pioneer among water theme parks, is much smaller but is very well done. Since Typhoon Lagoon opened in 1989, River Country has catered primarily to Walt Disney World campground and resort hotel guests. Blizzard Beach is the newest Disney water park and features more slides than the other two parks combined. All three parks are beautifully landscaped, with great attention to atmosphere and aesthetics. Typhoon Lagoon and Blizzard Beach have their own adjacent parking lots. River Country can be reached on foot by campground guests or on Disney boat or bus by others.

OTHER WALT DISNEY WORLD VENUES

Downtown Disney (Downtown Disney Marketplace, Pleasure Island, and Disney's West Side)

Downtown Disney is a large shopping, dining, and entertainment complex encompassing the Downtown Disney Marketplace on the east, the gated (i.e., admission required) Pleasure Island nighttime entertainment venue in the middle, and Disney's West Side on the west. Downtown Disney Marketplace is home to the largest Disney character merchandise store in the world, upscale resort-wear and specialty shops, and several restaurants, including the tacky but popular Rainforest Cafe. Pleasure Island, in addition to the gated attractions described below, offers several upscale restaurants. Disney's West Side, which opened in 1997, combines nightlife, shopping, dining, and entertainment. Dan Aykroyd's House of Blues serves Cajun/Creole dishes in its restaurant and electric blues in its music hall. Bongos, a Cuban nightclub and cafe created by Gloria and Emilio Estefan, offers Caribbean flavors and rhythms. Wolfgang Puck Cafe, sandwiched among pricey boutiques (including a three-level Virgin Records megastore) is the West Side's prestige eatery. In the entertainment department you'll find a 24-screen cinema; a permanent showplace for the extraordinary, 70-person cast of *Cirque du Soleil;*

and DisneyQuest, a high-tech, interactive virtual reality and electronic games venue. Downtown Disney can be accessed via Disney buses from most Walt Disney World locations.

Pleasure Island

Part of the Downtown Disney complex, Pleasure Island is a six-acre nighttime entertainment center where one cover charge gets a visitor into any of eight nightclubs. The clubs have different themes and feature a variety of shows and activities. Music ranges from pop-rock, to country and western, to jazz. For the more sedentary (or exhausted) there is an adjacent 24-screen movie complex, or for the hungry, several restaurants, including a much-hyped Planet Hollywood.

Disney's BoardWalk

Located near Epcot, Disney's BoardWalk is an idealized replication of an East Coast turn-of-the-century waterfront resort. Open all day, the BoardWalk features upscale restaurants, shops and galleries, a brew pub, an ESPN sports bar, a nightclub with dueling pianos (New Orleans Pat O'Brien's–style), and a swanky dance club. Although there is no admission fee for the Board-Walk per se, individual clubs levy a cover charge at night. In addition to the public facilities are a 378-room deluxe hotel and a 532-unit time-share development. The BoardWalk is within walking distance of the Epcot resorts and the International Gateway of the Epcot theme park. Boat transportation is available from Disney-MGM Studios, with buses serving other Disney World locations.

Disney's Wide World of Sports

Covering 200 acres, Disney's Wide World of Sports is a state-of-the-art competition and training facility consisting of a 7,500-seat ballpark, a field house, and venues for baseball, softball, tennis, track and field, beach volleyball, and 27 other sports. In addition to being the spring-training home of the Atlanta Braves, the complex hosts a mind-boggling calendar of professional and amateur competitions. Although Walt Disney World guests are welcome at the complex as paid spectators, none of the facilities are available for use by guests unless they are participants in a scheduled competition.

The Disney Institute and Disney University

The Disney Institute offers life-enriching learning experiences to Walt Disney World resort guests, while Disney University conducts professional-development courses for private groups and corporations. Both programs share the campus located near the Downtown Disney Marketplace and are connected to other Walt Disney World locations by Disney bus service.

DISNEYSPEAK POCKET TRANSLATOR

Although it may come as a surprise to many, Walt Disney World has its own somewhat peculiar language. Here are some of terms you are likely to bump into:

DisneySpeak	**English Definition**
Adventure	Ride
Attraction	Ride or theater show
Attraction Host	Ride operator
Audience	Crowd
Backstage	Behind the scenes, out of view of customers
Bull Pen	Queuing area
Cast Member	Employee
Character	Disney cartoon character impersonated by an employee
Costume	Work attire or uniform
Dark Ride	Indoor ride
Day Guest	Any customer not staying at a Disney resort
Face Character	A character that does not wear a head-covering costume (Snow White, Cinderella, Jasmine, etc.)
General Public	Same as day guest
Greeter	Employee positioned at the entrance of an attraction
Guest	Customer

DisneySpeak	**English Definition (continued)**
Hidden Mickeys	Frontal silhouette of Mickey's head worked subtly into the design of buildings, railings, vehicles, golf greens, attractions, and just about anything else
In Rehearsal	Operating, though not officially open
Lead	Foreman or manager, the person in charge of an attraction
On Stage	In full view of customers
Preshow	Entertainment at an attraction prior to the feature presentation
Resort Guest	A customer staying at a Disney resort
Role	An employee's job
Security Host	Security guard
Soft Opening	Opening a park or attraction before its stated opening time
Transitional Experience	An element of the queuing area and/or preshow that provides a story line or information essential to understanding the attraction

Part One

Basic Considerations

Is Walt Disney World for You?

Almost all people enjoy Walt Disney World on some level and find things to see and do that they like. In fact, for many, the theme park attractions are just the tip of the iceberg. The more salient question, then (since this is a family vacation), is whether the members of your family basically like the same things. If you do, fine. If not, how will you handle the differing agendas?

A mother from Toronto wrote a couple of years ago describing her husband's aversion to Disney's (in his terms) "phony, plastic and idealized version of life." Touring the theme parks, he was a real cynic and managed to diminish the experience for the rest of the family. As it happened, however, dad's pejorative point of view didn't extend to the Disney golf courses. So mom packed him up and sent him golfing while the family enjoyed the theme parks.

If you have someone in your family who doesn't like theme parks or who, for whatever reason, doesn't care for Disney's brand of entertainment, it helps to get the attitude out in the open. Our recommendation is to deal with the person up front. Glossing over or ignoring the contrary opinion and hoping that "Tom will like it once he gets there" is naive and unrealistic. Either leave Tom at home, or help him discover and plan activities that he will enjoy, resigning yourself in the process to the fact that the family won't be together at all times.

DIFFERENT FOLKS, DIFFERENT STROKES

It's no secret that we at the *Unofficial Guides* believe that thorough planning is an essential key to a successful Walt Disney World vacation. It's also no secret that our emphasis on planning rubs some folks the wrong way. The author's sister and her husband, for example, are very spontaneous people and do not appreciate the concept of detailed planning or, more particularly, following one of our touring plans when they visit the theme parks. To them the most important thing is to relax, take things as they come, and enjoy the moment. Sometimes they arrive at Epcot at 10:30 in the morning (impossibly late for us *Unofficial Guide* types), walk around enjoying the landscaping and architecture, and then sit with a cup of espresso watching *Unofficial Guide* readers race around the park like maniacs. They would be the first to admit that they don't see many attractions, but experiencing attractions is not what lights their sparklers.

Not coincidentally, most of our readers are big on planning. When they go to the theme park they want to experience the attractions, and the shorter the lines the better. In a word, they are willing to sacrifice some spontaneity for touring efficiency.

We want you to have the best possible time, whatever that means to you, so plan (or not) according to your preference. The point here is that most families (unlike my sister and her husband) are not entirely congruent on this planning versus spontaneity issue. If you are a serious planner and your oldest daughter and husband are free spirits, you've got the makings of a problem. In practice, the way this and similar scenarios shake out is that the planner (usually the more assertive party) just takes over. Sometimes daughter and husband go along and everything works out, but just as often they feel resentful. There are as many ways of developing a win/win compromise as there are well-intended people on different sides of this situation. How you settle it is up to you. We're simply suggesting that you examine the problem and work out the solution *before* you go on vacation.

TYPES OF PARENTS AND TYPES OF CHILDREN

Most parents try hard to do the best job they can with their children. However, ten minutes of observing parents and children in line for *Dumbo* will clearly reveal that some moms and dads have a greater aptitude for parenting than others.

Some parents are, for lack of a better word, naturals at the job. Every moment in the company of their children is treasured and enjoyed. These parents, who take everything in cheerful stride, view parenting as a happy, pleasant pastime. Their children are their best friends, the people whose company they enjoy most. Naturals understand that children have altered their lives, but view the alteration as an enhancement as opposed to an imposition or sacrifice. For these parents, the parent-child relationship is the cornerstone of family life, and the day-to-day life of the family is its logical function.

At the opposite end of the spectrum are those parents for whom every act is an effort, who feel oppressed by their parental responsibility and obligation, and who must really work at being a parent. These are the parents who preface their opinions with statements like, "I wouldn't trade my kids for anything in the world, but . . ." Usually parents who lack a real comfort level with children (their own as well as those of others), they are fully cognizant of, but never totally adjusted to, the way their children have changed their lives. Generally speaking, they are effective as parents and take "the job" very seriously, but derive minimal joy from parenting. They prefer the company of adults and create opportunities to "recharge their batteries" away from the kids. For these parents the parent-child relationship is somewhat tenuous, so family functionality is primarily achieved through the introduction of structure and rules. For the purpose of this discussion, we will call these parents "structuring parents."

In two-parent households, both parents might be cut from the same mold, be polar opposites, or (more likely) occupy a space on the parenting continuum somewhere in between. As a general rule, some fusion occurs that both incorporates and modifies the basic parenting type of the two individuals.

Kids, of course, also come in assorted personalities. In fact, I have always been amazed by the extent to which a child's basic personality manifests itself even as an infant. Even those who support the proposition that "there are no bad children, only bad parents" acknowledge that there is a genetic dimension to personality that, learned behaviors notwithstanding, makes some children more happy, easygoing, and mellow while others are more temperamental and difficult.

In the context of a Disney vacation, it is useful to locate your, your partner's, and your combined parenting type on the parenting continuum and your child's basic personality type on the personality continuum.

Parenting Type/Child Personality Continuum

Parenting Continuum
    Natural_____/_____Structuring

Child Personality Continuum
    Easygoing_____/_____Temperamental

If you and your partner are naturals and your child (or children) is easygoing, you could vacation on Mars and have a good time. At Walt Disney World, the most child-friendly of destinations, you'll coast right along. If your children are not altogether easygoing, a little advance planning and on-site attention to things like getting enough rest and not overloading the itinerary will keep things mellow.

Conversely, if you and your partner are structuring parents, your family will have to plan in greater detail and work harder to have a successful vacation. Because rules that apply at home are not applicable or are more difficult to administer while traveling, structuring parents often have a tough time rolling with the punches. If you have easygoing kids, Walt Disney World will be a nearly perfect vacation venue because the theme parks will provide much of the structure and organization that you work so hard to provide at home. You won't have to worry, for example, about what to do: Filling the hours and days will be snap. You'll also discover that Disney frames and structures the visits of all guests in subtle (and sometimes not so subtle) ways, ways that will remove much of the burden of initiating structure in adapting to the new environment.

If you are a structuring parent and your children are sometimes difficult, your best bet is to put Walt Disney World off for a few years. Older children, even somewhat temperamental ones, are better able to adjust to things not going their way than are younger children. Additionally, because older children are more independent and physically capable, they are able to function more completely in the adult-oriented world that structuring parents prefer.

Most parents, of course, are neither pure structuring nor natural, but fall somewhere in between. Analyzing your own parenting tendencies and style, however, provides some critical insight into how things are likely to work on vacation with different types of children.

In case you're wondering, the author is definitely *not* a natural. Even with really great kids he struggled a lot, and he struggles still. Once, however, in a moment of monumental clarity, he articulated an insight that has subsequently become known as "Sehlinger's Law." Although you've probably never heard of it, we'll bet you a pound cake to a penny that you are familiar with the experience. Sehlinger's Law postulates that "the number of adults required to take care of an active toddler is equal to the number of adults present, plus one."

THE NATURE OF THE BEAST

Though many parents don't realize it, there is no law that says you must take your kids to Walt Disney World. Likewise, there's no law that says you will enjoy Walt Disney World. And although we will help you make the most of any visit, we can't change the basic nature of the beast . . . er, mouse. A Walt Disney World vacation is an active and physically demanding undertaking. Regimentation, getting up early, lots of walking, waiting in lines, fighting crowds, and (often) enduring heat and humidity are as intrinsic to a Walt Disney World vacation as stripes are to a zebra. Especially if you're traveling with children, you'll need a sense of humor, more than a modicum of patience, and the ability to roll with the punches.

Clearly, we're not trying to dissuade you from vacationing at Walt Disney World with your children, but we want you to know what you're getting into. Simply put, you can enjoy a perfectly wonderful time in the World if you are realistic, organized, and prepared.

KNOW THYSELF AND NOTHING TO EXCESS

This good advice was made available to ancient Greeks courtesy of the oracle of Apollo at Delphi, who gave us permission to pass it along to you. First, concerning the "know thyself" part, we want you to do some serious thinking concerning what you want in a vacation. We also want you to entertain the notion that having fun and deriving pleasure from your vacation may be very different indeed from doing and seeing as much as possible.

Because Walt Disney World is expensive, many families confuse "seeing everything" in order to "get our money's worth" with having a great time. Sometimes the two are compatible, but more often they are not. So, if sleeping in, relaxing with the paper over coffee, sunbathing by the pool, or taking a nap rank high on your vacation hit parade, you need to accord them due emphasis on your Disney visit (are you listening?), even if it means you see less of the theme parks.

Which brings us to the "nothing to excess" part. At Walt Disney World, especially if you are touring with children, less is definitely more. Trust us, you cannot go full tilt dawn to dark in the theme parks day after day. First you'll get tired, then you'll get cranky, and then you'll adopt a production mentality ("we've got three more rides and then we can go back to the hotel"). Finally, you'll hit the wall because you just can't maintain the pace. So, get a grip on your needs and preferences before you leave home and develop an itinerary that incorporates all the things that make you happiest.

Plan on seeing Walt Disney World in bite-size chunks with plenty of sleeping, swimming, napping, and relaxing in between. Ask yourself over and over in both the planning stage and while you are at Walt Disney World, what will contribute the greatest contentedness, satisfaction, and harmony? Trust your instincts. If stopping for ice cream or returning to the hotel for a dip feels like more fun than seeing another attraction, do it—even if it means wasting the remaining hours of an expensive admissions pass.

The Age Thing

There is a lot of serious cogitation among parents and grandparents in regard to how old a child should be before embarking on a trip to Walt Disney World. The answer, not always obvious, stems from the personalities and maturity of the children, and the personalities and parenting style of the adults.

Walt Disney World for Infants and Toddlers

We believe that traveling with infants and toddlers is a great idea. Developmentally, travel is a stimulating learning experience for even the youngest of children. Infants, of course, will not know Mickey Mouse from a draft horse, but will respond to sun and shade, music, bright colors, and the extra attention they receive from you. From first steps to fully mobile at three years, children respond to the excitement and spectacle of Walt Disney World, though of course in a much different way than do you. Your toddler will prefer splashing in fountains and clambering over curbs and benches to experiencing most attractions, but no matter: He or she will still have a great time.

Somewhere between four and six years of age, your child will experience the first vacation that he or she will remember as an adult. Though more likely to remember the comfortable coziness of the hotel room than the theme parks, he or she will be able to experience and comprehend many attractions and will be a much fuller participant in your vacation. Even so, his or her favorite activity is likely to be swimming in the hotel pool.

As concerns infants and toddlers, there are good reasons and bad reasons for vacationing at Walt Disney World. A good reason for taking your little one to Walt Disney World is that you want to go and there's no one available to care for your child during your absence. Philosophically, we are very much against putting your life (including your vacation) on hold until your children are older. Traveling with infants and toddlers sharpens parenting skills and makes the entire family more mobile and flexible, resulting in a richer, fuller life for all.

Especially if you have children of varying ages (or plan to, for that matter) it's better to take the show on the road than to wait until the youngest reaches the perceived ideal age. If your family includes a toddler or infant, you will find everything from private facilities for breast feeding to changing tables in both men's and women's rest rooms to facilitate baby's care. Your whole family will be able to tour together with fewer hassles than on a day's picnic outing at home.

A bad reason, however, for taking an infant or toddler to Walt Disney World is that, through some misguided logic, you think Walt Disney World is the perfect vacation destination for babies.

Believe us, it's not, so think again if you are contemplating Walt Disney World primarily for your child's enjoyment. For starters, attractions are geared more toward older children and adults. Even designer play areas like Tom Sawyer Island in the Magic Kingdom are developed with older children in mind.

By way of example, the author has a friend who bought a video camcorder when his first child was born. He delighted in documenting his son's reaction to various new experiences on video. One memorable night when the baby was about 18 months old, he taped the baby eating a variety of foods (from whipped cream to dill pickles) that he had never tried before. While some of the taste sensations elicited wild expressions and animated responses from the baby, the exercise was clearly intended for the amusement of Dad, not junior. Likewise with Walt Disney World, you might score a few memorable photos for the scrapbook as your child reacts to the noise, crowds, and attractions, but don't fool yourself into thinking that the infant or toddler is getting much out of it.

Along similar lines, remember when you were little and you got that nifty electric train for Christmas, the one Dad wouldn't let you play with? Did you ever wonder who that train was really for? Ask yourself the same question about your vacation to Walt Disney World. Whose dream are you trying to make come true: yours or your child's?

If you elect to take your infant or toddler to Walt Disney World, rest assured that their needs have been anticipated. The major theme parks have centralized facilities for infant and toddler care. Everything necessary for changing diapers, preparing formula, and warming bottles and food is available. Baby supplies, including disposable diapers, formula, and baby food are for sale, and there are rockers and special chairs for nursing mothers. At the Magic Kingdom, the Baby Center is next to the Crystal Palace at the end of Main Street. At Epcot, Baby Services is near the Odyssey Center, right of Test Track in Future World. At Disney-MGM Studios, Baby Care is in the Guest Relations Building left of the entrance. At the Animal Kingdom, Baby Changing/Nursing is in Safari Village in the center of the park. Dads in charge of little ones are welcome at the centers and can use most services offered. In addition, many men's rooms in the major theme parks have changing tables.

Infants and toddlers are allowed to experience any attraction that doesn't have minimum height or age restrictions. But as a Minneapolis mother reports, some attractions are better for babies than others:

Theater and boat rides are easier for babies (ours was almost one year old, not yet walking). Rides where there's a bar that comes down are doable, but harder. Peter Pan was our first encounter with this type, and we had barely gotten situated when I realized he might fall out of my grasp. The standing auditorium films are too intense; the noise level is deafening, and the images inescapable. You don't have a rating system for babies, and I don't expect to see one, but I thought you might want to know what a baby thought (based on his reactions). [At the Magic Kingdom:] Jungle Cruise—Didn't get into it. Pirates— Slept through it. Riverboat—While at Aunt Polly's, the horn made him cry. Aunt Polly's—Ate the chicken while watching the birds in relative quiet. Small World—Wide-eyed, took it all in. Peter Pan—Couldn't really sit on the seat. A bit dangerous. He didn't get into it. Carousel of Progress—*Long talks; hard to keep him quiet; danced during song.* The Timekeeper—*Too loud. Dinosaur at beginning scared him. WDW RR—Liked the motion and scenery.* Tiki Birds—*Loved it. Danced, clapped, sang along. At Epcot:* Honey, I Shrunk the Audience—*We skipped due to recommendation of Disney worker that it got too loud and adults screamed throughout. Journey into Imagination—Loved it. Tried to catch things with his hands. Bounced up and down, chortled. The Land— Watchful, quiet during presentation.* Food Rocks— *Loved it, danced. El Río del Tiempo—Loved it.*

The same mom also advises:

We used a baby sling on our trip and thought it was great when standing in the lines—much better than a stroller, which you have to park before getting in line (and navigate through crowds). My baby was still nursing when we went to WDW. The only really great place I found to nurse in MK was a hidden bench in the shade in

Adventureland in between the freezee stand (next to Tiki Birds) and the small shops. It is impractical to go to the baby station every time, so a nursing mom better be comfortable about nursing in very public situations.

Two points in our reader's comment warrant elaboration. First, the rental strollers at all of the major theme parks are designed for toddlers and children up to three and four years old, but are definitely not for infants. Still, if you bring a supply of pillows and padding, the rental strollers can be made to work. And, in addition to providing an alternative to carrying your child, the stroller serves as a handy cart for diaper bags, water bottles, and other items you deem necessary to have on hand. You can alternatively bring your own stroller, but unless it's collapsible, you will not be able to take it on Disney trams, buses, or boats.

Even if you opt for a stroller (your own or a rental model), we nevertheless recommend that you also bring a baby sling or baby/child backpack. Simply put, there will be many times in the theme parks when you will have to park the stroller and carry your child. As an aside, if you haven't checked out baby slings and packs lately, you'll be amazed by some of the technological advances made in these products.

The second point that needs addressing is our reader's perception that there are not many good places in the theme parks for breast feeding unless you are accustomed to nursing in public. Many nursing moms recommend breast feeding during a dark Disney theater presentation. This only works, however, if the presentation is long enough for the baby to finish nursing. *The Hall of Presidents* at the Magic Kingdom and *The American Adventure* at Epcot will afford you about 23 and 29 minutes, respectively. In addition, neither production includes noise or special effects that will frighten your infant, although you can expect fairly loud volume levels for narration and music. *Impressions de France* in the French pavilion at Epcot's World Showcase is only 18 minutes long, but is very quiet and relaxing. For the time being, unfortunately, there are no theater presentations at the Animal Kingdom that offer sufficient quiet and adequate time to nurse. At the Disney-MGM Studios, *Voyage of the Little Mermaid* will work if your child can get filled up in 15 minutes.

If you can adjust to nursing in more public places with your breast and the baby's head covered with a shawl or some such, nursing will not be a problem at all. Even on the most crowded days, you can always find a back corner of a restaurant or a comparatively secluded park bench or garden spot to nurse. Finally, the baby centers, with their private nursing rooms, are centrally located in all of the parks except the Disney-MGM Studios.

Walt Disney World for Four-, Five-, and Six-Year-Olds

Four-, five-, and six-year-olds vary immensely in their capacity to comprehend and enjoy Walt Disney World. With this age group the go/no-go decision is a judgment call. If your child is sturdy, easygoing, fairly adventuresome, and demonstrates a high degree of independence, the trip will probably work. On the other hand, if your child tires easily, is temperamental, is a bit timid or reticent in embracing new experiences, or has a short umbilicus, you're much better off waiting a few years. Where the travel and sensory-overload problems of infants and toddlers can be addressed and (usually) remedied on the go, discontented four- to six-year-olds have the ability to stop a family dead in its tracks, as this mother of three from Cape May, New Jersey, attests:

> *My five-year-old was scared pretty bad on* Snow White *our first day at Disney World. From then on for the rest of the trip we had to coax and reassure her before each and every ride before she would go. It was like pulling teeth.*

If you have a retiring, clinging, and/or difficult four- to six-year-old who, for whatever circumstances, will be part of your group, you can sidestep or diminish potential problems with a bit of pretrip preparation. Even if your preschooler is plucky and game, the same prep measures (described later in this section) will enhance his or her experience and make life easier for the rest of the family.

The Ideal Age

Although our readers report both successful trips as well as disasters with children of all ages, the consensus ideal children's ages for family compatibility and togetherness at Walt Disney World are 8 to 12 years. This age group is old enough, tall enough, and sufficiently stalwart to experience, understand, and appreciate practically all Disney attractions. Moreover, they are developed to the extent that they can get around the parks on their own steam without being carried or collapsing. Best of all, they are still young enough to enjoy being with mom and dad. From our experience, ages 10 to 12 are better than 8 and 9, though what you gain in maturity is at the cost of that irrepressible, wide-eyed wonder so prevalent in the 8- and 9-year-olds.

Walt Disney World for Teens

Teens love Walt Disney World, and for parents of teens the "World" is a nearly perfect, albeit expensive vacation choice. Although your teens might not be as wide-eyed and impressionable as their younger sibs, they are at an age where they can sample, understand, and enjoy practically everything Walt Disney World has to offer—and we do mean *everything*. Teens for example, delight in playing adult at Pleasure Island, Walt Disney World's nighttime entertainment complex, hopping from club to club (teens and even younger children are eligible for admission to most Disney night clubs, but are not allowed to purchase alcohol).

For parents, Walt Disney World is a vacation destination where you can permit your teens an extraordinary amount of freedom. The entertainment is wholesome, the venues are safe, and the entire complex of hotels, theme parks, restaurants, and shopping centers are accessible via the Walt Disney World transportation system. The transportation system allows you, for example, to enjoy a romantic dinner and an early bedtime while your teens take in the late night fireworks at the theme parks. After the fireworks, a Disney bus, boat, or monorail will deposit them safely back at the hotel.

Because most adolescents relish freedom, you may have difficulty keeping your teens with the rest of the family. Thus, if one of your objectives is to spend time with your teenage children during your Disney World vacation, you will need to establish some clear-cut guidelines regarding togetherness and separateness before you leave home. Make your teens part of the discussion and try to meet them halfway in crafting a decision everyone can live with. For your teens, touring on their own at Walt Disney World is tantamount to being independent in a large city. It's intoxicating, to say the least, and can be an excellent learning experience, if not a rite of passage. In any event, we're not suggesting that you just turn them loose. Rather, we are just attempting to sensitize you to the fact that for your teens, there are some transcendent issues involved.

Most teens crave the company of other teens. If you have a solitary teen in your family, do not be surprised if he or she wants to invite a friend on your vacation. If you are invested in sharing intimate, quality time with your solitary teen, the presence of a friend will make this difficult, if not impossible. However, if you turn down the request to bring a friend, be prepared to go the extra mile to be a companion to your teen at Walt Disney World. Expressed differently, if you're a teen, it's not much fun to ride Space Mountain by yourself.

One specific issue that absolutely should be addressed before you leave home is what assistance (if any) you expect from your teen in regard to helping with younger children in the family. Once again, try to carve out a win/win compromise. Consider the case of the mother from Indiana who had a teenage daughter from an earlier marriage and two children under age ten from a second marriage. After a couple of vacations where she thrust the unwilling teen into the position of being a surrogate parent to her stepsisters, the teen declined henceforth to participate in family vacations.

Many parents have written the *Unofficial Guide* asking if there are unsafe places at Walt Disney World or places where teens simply should not be allowed to go. Although the answer depends more on your family values and the relative maturity of your teens than on Walt Disney World, the basic answer is no. Though it's true that teens (or adults, for that matter) who are looking for trouble can find it anywhere, there is absolutely nothing at Walt Disney World that could be construed as a precipitant or a catalyst. Be advised, however, that adults consume alcohol at most Walt Disney World restaurants and that drinking is a very visible part of the Pleasure Island club scene. Also, be aware that some of the movies available at the cinemas at the West Side of Downtown Disney demand the same discretion you exercise when allowing your kids to see movies at home.

If, as a final aside, you allow your teens some independence and they are getting around on the Walt Disney World transportation system, expect some schedule slippage. There are no posted transportation schedules other than when service begins in the morning and when service terminates at night. Thus, to catch a bus, for example, you just go to a bus station and wait for the next bus to your Disney World destination. If you happen to just miss the bus, you might have to wait 15 to 45 minutes (more often 15 to 20 minutes) for the next one. If punctuality is essential, advise your independent teens to arrive at a transportation station an hour before they are expected somewhere in order to allow sufficient time for the commute.

About Inviting Your Children's Friends

If your children want to invite friends on your Walt Disney World vacation, give your decision careful thought: There's more involved here than might be apparent. First, consider the logistics of numbers. Is there room in the car? Will you have to leave something at home that you had planned on taking to make room in the trunk for the friend's luggage? Will additional hotel rooms or a larger condo be required? Will the increased number of people in your group make it hard to get a table at a restaurant?

If you determine that you can logistically accommodate one or more friends, the next step is to consider how the inclusion of the friend will affect your group's dynamics. Generally speaking, the presence of a friend will make it harder to really connect with your own children. So if one of your vacation goals is an intimate bonding experience with your children, the addition of friends will probably frustrate your attempts to realize that objective.

If family relationship building is not necessarily a primary objective of your vacation, it's quite possible that the inclusion of a friend will make life easier for you. This is especially true in the case of only children, who may otherwise depend exclusively on you to keep them happy and occupied. Having a friend along can take the pressure off and give you some much-needed breathing room.

If you decide to allow a friend to accompany you, limit the selection to children you know really well and whose parents you also know. Your Walt Disney World vacation is not the time to include "my friend Eddie from school" whom you've never met. Your children's friends who have spent time in your home will have a sense of your parenting style, and you will have a sense of their personality, behavior, and compatibility with your family. Assess the prospective child's potential to fit in well on a long trip. Is he or she polite, personable, fun to be with, and reasonably mature? Does he or she relate well to you and to the other members of your family?

Because a Walt Disney World vacation is not, for most of us, a spur-of-the-moment thing, you should have adequate time to evaluate potential candidate friends. A trip to the mall including a meal in a sit-down restaurant will tell you volumes about the friend. Likewise, inviting the friend to share dinner with the family and then spend the night will provide a lot of relevant information. Ideally this type of evaluation should take place early on in the normal course of family events, before you discuss the possibility of a friend joining you on your vacation. This will allow you to size things up without your child (or the friend) realizing that an evaluation is taking place.

By seizing the initiative, you can guide the outcome. A Springfield, Ohio, mom named Ann, for example, anticipated that her 12-year-old son would ask to take a friend on their vacation. As she pondered the various friends her son might propose, she came up with four names. One, an otherwise sweet child, had a medical condition that Ann felt unqualified to monitor or treat. A second friend was overly aggressive with younger children and was often socially inappropriate for his age. Two other friends, Chuck and Marty, with whom she had had a generally positive experience, were good candidates for the trip. After orchestrating some opportunities to spend time with each of the boys, she made her decision and asked her son, "Would you like to take Marty with us to Disney World?" Her son was delighted, and Ann had diplomatically preempted having to turn down friends her son might have proposed.

We recommend that *you* do the inviting, instead of your child, and that the invitation be extended parent to parent. Observing this process will allow you to query the friend's parents concerning food preferences, any medical conditions, how discipline is administered in the friend's family, how the friend's parents feel about the way you administer discipline, and the parents' expectation regarding religious observations while their child is in your care.

Before you extend the invitation, give some serious thought to who pays for what. Make a specific proposal for financing the trip a part of your invitation, for example, "There's room for Marty in the hotel room, and transportation's no problem because we're driving. So we'll just need you to pick up Marty's meals, theme park admissions, and spending money." As an aside, we suggest that you arrange for the friend's parents to reimburse you after the trip for things like restaurant meals and admissions. This is much easier than trying to balance the books after every expenditure.

A Few Words for Single Parents

Because single parents generally are also working parents, planning a special getaway with your children can be the best way to spend some quality time together. But remember, the vacation is not just for your child—it's for you, too. You might invite a grandparent or a favorite aunt or uncle along; the other adult provides nice company for you, and your child will benefit from the time with family members.

Don't try to spend every moment with your children on vacation. Instead, plan some activities for your children with other children. Disney educational programs for children, for example, are worth considering. Then take advantage of your free time to do what you want to do: Read a book, have a massage, take a long walk or a catnap.

"He Who Hesitates Is Launched!" Tips and Warnings for Grandparents

Seniors often get into predicaments caused by touring with grandchildren. Run ragged and pressured to endure a blistering pace, many seniors just concentrate on surviving Walt Disney World rather than enjoying it. The theme parks have as much to offer older visitors as they do children, and seniors must either set the pace or dispatch the young folks to tour on their own.

An older reader from Alabaster, Alabama, writes:

> The main thing I want to say is that being a senior is not
> for wussies. At Disney World particularly, it requires
> courage and pluck. Things that used to be easy take a lot

> *of effort, and sometimes your brain has to wait for your*
> *body to catch up. Half the time, your grandchildren treat*
> *you like a crumbling ruin and then turn around and*
> *trick you into getting on a roller coaster in the dark. What*
> *you need to tell seniors is that they have to be alert and*
> *not trust anyone. Not their children or even the Disney*
> *people, and especially not their grandchildren. When your*
> *grandchildren want you to go on a ride, don't follow along*
> *blindly like a lamb to the slaughter. Make sure you know*
> *what the ride is all about. Stand your ground and do not*
> *waffle. He who hesitates is launched!*

If you don't get to see much of your grandchildren, you might think that Walt Disney World is the perfect place for a little bonding and togetherness. Wrong! Walt Disney World sends children into system overload and precipitates behaviors that pose a challenge even to adoring parents, never mind grandparents. You don't take your grandchildren straight to Disney World for the same reason you don't buy your 16-year-old son a Ferrari: Handling it safely and well requires a lot of experience.

Begin by spending time with your grandchildren in an environment that you can control. Have them over one at a time for dinner and to spend the night. Check out how they respond to your oversight and discipline. Most of all, zero in on whether you are compatible, enjoy each other's company, and have fun together. Determine that you can set limits and that they will accept those limits. When you reach this stage you can contemplate some outings to the zoo, to the movies, shopping, or to the state fair. Gauge how demanding your grandchildren are when you are out of the house. Eat a meal or two in a full-service restaurant to get a sense of their social skills and their ability to behave appropriately. Don't expect perfection, and be prepared to modify your behavior a little, too. As a senior friend of mine told her husband (none too decorously), "You can't see Walt Disney World sitting on a stick."

If you have a good relationship with your grandchildren and have had a positive one-on-one experience taking care of them, you might consider a trip to Walt Disney World. If you do, we have two recommendations. First, visit Walt Disney World without them to get an idea of what you're getting into. A scouting trip will also provide you an opportunity to enjoy some of the attractions that won't be on the itinerary when you return with the grandkids. Second, if you are considering a trip of a week's duration, you might think about buying a Disney package that combines four days at Walt Disney World with a three-day cruise on the *Disney Magic* or the *Disney Wonder*. In addition to being a memorable experience for your grandchildren, the cruise provides plenty of structure for children of almost every age, thus allowing you to be with them, but also to have some time for yourselves. Call the Disney Cruise Line at (407) 939-3727 or visit the Web site at *www.disneycruise.com.*

A Dozen Additional Tips for Grandparents

1. It's best to take one grandchild at a time, two at the most. Cousins can be better than siblings because they don't fight as much.

2. Let your grandchildren help plan the vacation, and keep the first one short. Be flexible, and don't overplan.

3. Discuss mealtimes and bedtime. Fortunately, many grandparents are on an early dinner schedule, which works nicely with younger children. Also, if you want to plan a special evening out, be sure to make the reservation ahead of time.

4. Gear plans to your grandchildren's age levels, because if they're not happy, you won't be happy.

5. Create an itinerary that offers some supervised activities for children in case you need a rest.

6. If you're traveling by car, this is the one time we highly recommend headphones. Kids' musical tastes are vastly different from most grandparents', and it's simply more enjoyable when everyone can listen to his or her own preferred style of music.

7. Take along a nightlight.

8. Carry a notarized statement from parents for permission for medical care in case of an emergency. Also be sure you have insurance information and copies of any prescriptions for medicines the kids may be on. Ditto for eyeglass prescriptions.

9. Tell your grandchildren about any medical problems you may have so they can be prepared if there's an emergency.

10. Many attractions and hotels offer discounts for seniors, so be sure you check ahead of time for bargains.

11. Plan your evening meal early to avoid long waits. And make priority seating arrangements if you're dining in a popular spot, even if it's early. Stash some crayons and paper in your bag to keep kids occupied.

12. If planning a family-friendly trip seems overwhelming, try Grandtravel (call (800) 247-7651), a tour operator–travel agent aimed at kids and their grandparents.

Part Two

Getting Your Act Together

Gathering Information

In addition to this guide, we recommend that you obtain:

1. The Walt Disney Travel Company Walt Disney World Vacations Brochure   This full-color booklet describes Walt Disney World in its entirety, lists rates for all Disney resort hotels and campgrounds, and describes Walt Disney World package vacations. It's available from most travel agents or by calling the Walt Disney Travel Company at (800) 327-2996 or (407) 828-3232. Be prepared to hold; you may have a long wait.

2. Walt Disney World Guidebook for Guests with Disabilities   If members of your party are sight- or hearing-impaired, or partially or wholly nonambulatory, this small guide will be very helpful. For a copy, call (407) 824-4321. Allow 15 business days for delivery.

3. Orlando MagiCard   If you're considering lodging outside Walt Disney World or if you think you might patronize attractions and restaurants outside Disney World, it's worthwhile to obtain an Orlando MagiCard, a Vacation Planner, and the Orlando Official Accommodations Guide (all free) from the Orlando/Orange County Convention and Visitors Bureau. The MagiCard makes you eligible for discounts at hotels, restaurants, and attractions outside Disney World. To order the accommodations guide, call (800) 255-5786. For additional information and materials, call (407) 363-5874. Phones are staffed during weekday business hours. Allow 4 weeks for delivery.

4. Florida Traveler Discount Guide   Another good source of discounts on lodging, restaurants, and attractions throughout the state is the Florida Traveler Discount Guide. Published by Exit Information Guide, the guide is free, but you will be charged $3 ($5 if shipped to Canada) for handling. Call (352) 371-3948, 8 a.m.–8 p.m. EST Monday–Friday. Similar guides to other states are available at the same number. It's sometimes difficult to get through on the phone, however.

5. Kissimmee–St. Cloud Tour & Travel Sales Guide   This full-color directory of hotels and attractions is one of the most complete available and is of particular interest to those who intend to book lodging outside of Walt Disney World. In addition to hotels and motels, the directory lists rental houses, time-shares, and condominiums. To receive a copy, call the Kissimmee–St. Cloud Convention and Visitors Bureau at (800) 327-9159.

6. *The Eclectic Gourmet Guide to Orlando*   If you plan to eat a lot of restaurant meals, this guide by the creators of the *Unofficial Guide* series will help you find the best dining Orlando and Walt Disney World have to offer. The 220-page book, which rates and ranks more than 150 restaurants, is available for $11.95 plus shipping by calling (800) 247-9473.

REQUEST INFORMATION EARLY

Request information as far in advance as possible, and allow four weeks for delivery. Make a checklist of information you have requested and follow up if you haven't received your materials within six weeks.

GATHERING INFORMATION ON THE WORLD WIDE WEB

In planning your Walt Disney World vacation, you will find all of your favorite characters on the World Wide Web. But in addition to Mickey, Minnie, Donald, Pluto, and Goofy, you will also find Delta, American, Hertz, Hyatt, and Hilton. Searching the Web for Disney information is like navigating an immense maze for a very small piece of cheese. To be sure, there is a lot of information available on the Web, but you may have to wade through list after list until you find the Internet addresses you want and need. Once you have the addresses you want, finding information can also be time consuming.

Disney's official Web page offers much of the same information as the Walt Disney Travel Company's vacation guidebook, and the guidebook has better pictures. However, the Web page is updated daily, contains some other useful information, and offers a few services. You can now purchase theme park admissions and make resort and dining reservations on the Internet. The Web page also offers online shopping, weather forecasts, and information on renovations and special events. Disney's official company home page address is *www.disney.com.* Universal Studios Florida also offers a home page at *www.usf.com.*

If you search for additional information, you will find that there are many private individuals who maintain very elaborate Disney-related Web pages. Private individuals also maintain Disney chat groups, which can be sources of both information and misinformation, depending on who is chatting. Disneyphile techies from all over the world help maintain lists. There are lists of hidden Mickeys, lists of attractions ranked and rated, lists of organizations that have a bone to pick with Disney, lists of characters, and more lists of lists. You could explore the Web for weeks on end for myriad information maintained by private individuals. Although a lot of this information is fun and interesting, and some is useful, the best way to get specific, detailed information without too long a wait is to call Disney's main information phone number: (407) 824-4321. Alternately, if you are looking for an evening's entertainment, try the Web.

Important Walt Disney World Addresses

Walt Disney World Info/Guest Letters/Letters to
Mickey Mouse
P.O. Box 10040
Lake Buena Vista, FL 32830-0040

Walt Disney World Central Reservations
P.O. Box 10100
Lake Buena Vista, FL 32830-0100

Important Walt Disney World Addresses (continued)

Walt Disney World Educational Programs
P.O. Box 10000
Lake Buena Vista, FL 32830-1000

Walt Disney World Ticket Mail Order
P.O. Box 10140
Lake Buena Vista, FL 32830-0140

Compliments, Complaints, and Suggestions
Walt Disney World Guest Communications
P. O. Box 10000
Lake Buena Vista, FL 32830-1000

IMPORTANT WALT DISNEY WORLD TELEPHONE NUMBERS

When you call the main information number at Walt Disney World, you will be offered a menu of options for recorded information on theme park operating hours, recreation areas, shopping, entertainment complexes, tickets and admissions, resort reservations, and directions by highway and from the airport. If you are using a rotary telephone, your call will be forwarded to a Disney information representative. If you are using a touch-tone phone and have a question not covered by recorded information, press eight (8) at any time to speak to a Disney representative.

Important Phone Numbers

General Information	(407) 824-4321
Accommodations/Reservations	(407) 934-7639
Dining Priority Seating	(407) 939-3463
Disney Institute Programs	(800) 746-5858
Disney's Wide World of Sports	(407) 363-6600
Golf Reservations and Information	(407) WDW-GOLF
Guided Tour Information	(407) 939-TOUR

Important Phone Numbers (continued)	
Lost and Found for articles lost:	
Yesterday or before	
(All parks)	(407) 824-4245
Today at Magic Kingdom	(407) 824-4521
Today at Epcot	(407) 560-6105
Today at Disney-MGM	(407) 560-3720
Today at Animal Kingdom	(407) 938-2265
Mediclinic, US 192,	
Kissimmee	(407) 239-1195
Walt Disney Travel Company	(407) 828-3232
Weather Information	(407) 824-4104
Wrecker Service	(407) 352-0842

Allocating Time

During Walt Disney World's first decade, a family with a week's vacation could enjoy the Magic Kingdom and River Country and still have several days for the beach or other local attractions. Since Epcot opened in 1982, however, Disney World has steadily been enlarging to monopolize the family's entire week. Today, with the addition of Blizzard Beach, Typhoon Lagoon, Disney-MGM Studios, the Animal Kingdom, and Downtown Disney, you should allocate six days for a whirlwind tour (seven to ten days if you're old-fashioned and insist on a little relaxation during your vacation). If you don't have six or more days, or think you might want to venture beyond the edge of "The World," be prepared to make some hard choices.

A seemingly obvious point lost on many families is that Walt Disney World is not going anywhere. There's no danger that it will be packed up and shipped to Iceland anytime soon. This means that you can come back if you don't see everything this year. Disney has planned it this way, of course, but it doesn't matter. It's infinitely more sane to resign yourself to the reality that seeing everything during one visit is impossible. We recommend, therefore, that you approach Walt Disney World the same way you would an eight-course Italian dinner: leisurely, with plenty of time between courses. The best way not to have fun is to cram too much into too little time.

WHEN TO GO TO WALT DISNEY WORLD

Let's cut to the essence: Walt Disney World between June 12 and August 18 is absolutely brutal. You can count on mind-boggling crowds as well as stupefying heat and humidity. Avoid these dates if you can. Ditto for Memorial Day weekend at the beginning of the summer and Labor Day weekend at the end. Other holiday periods (Thanksgiving, Christmas, Easter, spring break, and so on) are extremely crowded, but the heat is not as bad.

The best time to visit Walt Disney World is in the fall, especially November before Thanksgiving and December before Christmas. January after New Year's Day and February excluding national holidays are also good, although the weather is generally not as nice as it is in the fall. March and April bring spring break and Easter crowds, though it is sometimes possible (depending on the school and liturgical calendars) to find certain weeks in this period that are not too busy. Late April and May as well as the beginning of June are pretty good crowd-wise, but are hot and often rainy. Crowds in late August are more tolerable than the heat.

So, parents, what to do? If your children are preschool age, definitely go during a cooler less crowded time of year. If you have school-age children, look first for an anomaly in your school-year schedule: in other words, a time when your kids will be out of school when most other schools are in session. Anomalies are most often found at the beginning or end of the school year (for example, school starts late or lets out early), at Christmas, or at spring break. In the event that no such anomalies exist, and providing that your kids are good students, our recommendation is to ask permission to take your children out of school either just before or after the Thanksgiving holiday. Teachers can assign lessons that can be made up at home over the Thanksgiving holiday, either before or after your Walt Disney World vacation.

If none of the foregoing is workable for your family, consider visiting Walt Disney World the week immediately before school starts (excluding Labor Day weekend) or the week immediately after school lets out (excluding Memorial Day weekend). This strategy should remove you from the really big mob scenes by about a week.

If you are left with the choice of going during the hot, busy summer or not going at all, take heart. You can still have a good time, but you will probably see less and return more exhausted. Battling both heat and crowds at Walt Disney World is like fighting a war on two fronts. If you elect to go this route, visit as early in June or as late in August as possible, avoiding July like the plague. Set up your touring itinerary to visit the parks early in the morning and late in the evening with swimming and napping in between. Cut your visit short by one or two days so that you will have the weekend or a couple of vacation days remaining when you get home to recuperate.

Though we strongly recommend going to Walt Disney World at less busy times of year, you should know that there are trade-offs. The parks often open late and close early on fall, winter, and spring days. When they open as late as 10 a.m., everyone arrives about the same time, making it hard to beat the crowd. A late opening coupled with an early closing drastically reduces the hours available to tour. Even when crowds are small, it's difficult to see a big park like the Magic Kingdom or Epcot between 10 a.m. and 6 p.m. Early closing (before 8 p.m.) also usually means that evening parades or fireworks are eliminated. And, because these are slow times at Disney World, some rides and attractions may be closed for maintenance or renovation. Finally, central Florida temperatures fluctuate wildly during the late fall, winter, and early spring; daytime lows in the 40s are not uncommon.

Walt Disney World and the Millennium

Walt Disney World plans to celebrate the millennium for 15 months, from October 1999 until January 1st, 2001. Disney's millennium plans will manifest themselves in special versions of *IllumiNations* at Epcot, of *Fantasmic!* at the Disney-MGM Studios, and of parades, fireworks, and live entertainment at all the parks. Each park will herald a new attraction for the millennium. At Epcot it will be the new ride at the Imagination pavilion along with a sort of World's Fair Millenniun exhibit hall situated between England and Canada in the World Showcase. The Studios will unveil the new Rock 'n' Roller Coaster, and the Magic Kingdom will showcase its Winnie the Pooh ride in Fantasyland. At the Animal Kingdom the new rage is a stage show combining elements of a rock concert and the X-Games under the unlikely umbrella of a Tarzan theme (I promise I'm not making this up). Gratefully, there's no move afoot to disguise Cinderella Castle as a giant birthday cake (as was done for Walt Disney World's 25th anniversary celebration) or the Tree of Life as a humongous candelabra.

Disney's millennium press and advertising blitz will be in full swing by the time you read this guide, and you can bet that it will wrap its tentacles around any brain in America that's not comatose or on drugs. Disney promotional campaigns are usually pretty effective, so the salient point is that you can expect larger than usual crowds throughout the 15-month celebration. Year after year we hammer you about the benefits of visiting Walt Disney World during the off season, but this year the advice is more important than ever.

Selecting the Day of the Week for Your Visit

The only way stay ahead of the crowd is to start the day ahead of it. Sounds simple enough, but there's a complication: Disney allows its resort guests to enter a specific theme park each day one and a half hours early. So, if you're not a Disney resort guest, call (407) 824-4321, find out which park is scheduled for early entry, and avoid it (that is, spend the day at one of the other parks). If you are staying in a Disney hotel, you are eligible to take advantage of the early entry privilege, but be forewarned that the park that opens early will be the most crowded park on that particular day. If you have early entry privileges we recommend using them first thing in the morning and then moving on to another park when things get crowded (about 10 a.m.); alternately, avoid the early entry park altogether. The best time of year to use early entry privileges are during the less busy times of the year, when the parks are operating on abbreviated hours. During these periods early entry will add a couple of hours of extra touring time to an already short day.

Least-Crowded Days		

Holidays excepted, here are the least crowded days of the week for each major theme park:

	Summer	Fall, Winter, and Spring
Magic Kingdom	Sunday and Friday	Tuesday and Wednesday
Animal Kingdom	Thursday, Friday or Sunday	Thursday, Friday or Sunday
Epcot	Saturday and Sunday	Monday, Wednesday, Thursday
Disney-MGM Studios	Monday and Friday	Monday and Tuesday

Planning Your Walt Disney World Vacation Budget

How much you spend depends on how long you stay at Walt Disney World. But even if you only stop by for an afternoon, be prepared to drop a bundle. Later we'll show you how to save money on lodging. This section will give you some sense of what you can expect to pay for admissions and food. And we'll help you decide which admission option will best meet your needs.

ADMISSION OPTIONS

There are basically ten Walt Disney World admission options (many with silly names), but several of them are endangered species:

Type of Pass	Adult Price w/ Tax	Child Price w/ Tax
1-Day/One Park Only Pass	$47	$37
1-Day/One-Park Bounce-Back Pass	$36–42	$30–33
4-Day Park Hopper Pass	$177	$142
5-Day Park Hopper Pass	$210	$168

Type of Pass (continued)	Adult Price w/ Tax	Child Price w/ Tax
5-Day Park Hopper Plus Pass	$243	$194
6-Day Park Hopper Plus Pass	$275	$220
7-Day Park Hopper Plus Pass	$306	$245
Unlimited Magic Pass	*Varies according to length of stay*	
Annual Passports*	$328–387	$275–334
Florida Resident/Seasonal	$169	$144

* More expensive Annual Passports include water parks, Pleasure Island, and Disney's Wide World of Sports

Which Admission Should You Buy?

If you only have one day at Walt Disney World, select the park that most interests you and buy the 1-Day/One-Park Only Ticket. If you have two days and don't plan to return to Florida for a couple of years, buy two 1-Day tickets (or an Unlimited Magic Pass if you're a Disney lodging guest). If you think you might pass through the area again in the next year or two, spring for a 4-, 5-, 6-, or 7-Day pass. Use two days of admission to see as much as you can, and save the remaining days for another trip.

If you plan to spend three or more days at Walt Disney World, buy a 4- or 5-Day pass. If you live in Florida or plan to spend seven or more days in the major theme parks, the Annual Passport is a good buy. If you live in Florida and don't mind being restricted to visiting Walt Disney World at designated off-peak times, the Florida Resident's Seasonal Pass should be considered.

If you visit Walt Disney World every year, here's how to save big bucks. Let's say you usually take your vacation during summer. This year, plan your Disney vacation for July and buy an Annual Passport. Next year, go in June. Because Annual Passports start on the date of purchase, those you buy this year will still be good for next year's vacation if you go a month earlier! If you spend four days each year at Disney World (eight days in the two consecutive years), you'll cut your daily admission to about $36 per adult per day. The longer your Disney vacation, of course, the more you save with the Annual Passport. If you visit the theme parks seven days each year, your admission will be less than $21 per day. As a bonus, Annual Passports qualify you for big discounts at Disney resorts.

Admission Discounts

At Disney World as at Wal-Mart, volume rules. If you buy a 5-Day pass, you will pay less per day than if you buy a 1-Day or 4-Day pass. Admission discounts ranging between 3% and 5% are available to Magic Kingdom Gold Card holders, AAA members, and Disney time-share owners.

Old Passports and the Animal Kingdom

Unused days on multiday passports sold before the Animal Kingdom opened in 1998 are good only for the other three parks. In other words, you can't use them for admission to the Animal Kingdom.

FOOD

Every time you buy a soda at the theme parks it's going to set you back about $2, and everything else from hot dogs to salad is comparably high. You can say, "Oh well, we're on vacation," and pay the exorbitant prices, or you can plan ahead and save big bucks. For comparison purposes, let's say that a family of two adults and two young teens arrives at Walt Disney World on Sunday afternoon and departs for home the following Saturday after breakfast. During that period the family eats six breakfasts, five lunches, and six dinners. What those meals cost, of course, depends on where and what they eat. It is possible for them to rent a condo and prepare all of their own meals, but they didn't travel all the way to Walt Disney World to cook. So, let's be realistic and assume that they will eat their evening meals out (this is what most families do, because, among other reasons, they're too tired to think about cooking). It may be just burgers or pizza, but they eat dinner in a restaurant.

That leaves breakfast and lunch to contend with. Here, basically, are the options. Needless to say, there are dozens of other various combinations. They could eat all of their meals in full-service restaurants, for example, but the bottom line is that most people don't, so we'll just keep this relatively simple.

1. Eat breakfast in their room out of their cooler or fridge and prepare sandwiches and snacks to take to the theme parks in their hip packs. Carry water bottles or rely on

drinking fountains for water. Cost: $104 for family of four for six days (does not include dinners or food purchased on travel days)

2. Eat breakfast in their room out of their cooler or fridge, carry snacks in their hip packs, and buy lunch at Disney counter-service restaurants. Cost: $216 for family of four for six days (does not include dinners or food purchased on travel days)

3. Eat breakfast at their hotel restaurant, buy snacks from vendors, and eat lunch at Disney counter-service restaurants. Cost: $412 for family of four for six days (does not include dinners or food purchased on travel days)

In case you're wondering, these are the foods on which we've based our grocery costs for those options where breakfast, lunch, and/or snacks are prepared from the cooler:

Breakfast   Cold cereal (choice of two), breakfast pastries, bananas, orange juice, milk, and coffee.

Lunch   Cold cuts (sliced ham or turkey) or peanut butter and jelly sandwiches, condiments (mayo, mustard, and so on), boxed juice, apples.

Snacks   Packaged cheese or peanut butter crackers, boxed juice, and trail mix (combination of M&Ms, nuts, raisins, and so on).

If you opt to buy groceries, you can stock up on food for your cooler at the Publix Supermarket on the corner of FL 535 and Vineland Road. A second, more upscale (and pricier) store is the Goodings Supermarket in the Disney-owned Crossroads Shopping Center on FL 535 opposite the entrance to the Disney Hotel Plaza and Downtown Disney.

Projected costs for snacks purchased at the theme parks are based on drinks (coffee or sodas) twice a day and popcorn once each day. Counter-service meal costs assume basic meals (hot dogs, burgers, fries, and soda or coffee). Hotel breakfast expense assumes eggs, bacon, and toast, or pancakes with bacon, and juice, milk, or coffee to drink.

How Much Does It Cost per Day at Walt Disney World?

A typical day would cost $371.55, excluding lodging and transportation, for a family of four—Mom, Dad, 12-year-old Tim, and 8-year-old Sandy—driving their own car and staying outside of Walt Disney World. They plan to be in the area for a week, so they buy 5-Day Park-Hopper Passes. Here's a breakdown:

How Much Does a Day Cost?

Breakfast for four at Denny's with tax & tip	$25.50
Epcot parking fee	$5.00
One day's admission on a 5-Day Park-Hopper Pass	
Dad: Adult 5-Day with tax = $210 divided by five (days)	$42
Mom: Adult 5-Day with tax = $210 divided by five (days)	$42
Tim: Adult 5-Day with tax = $210 divided by five (days)	$42
Sandy: Child 5-Day with tax = $168 divided by five (days)	$33.60
Morning break (soda or coffee)	$7.00
Fast-food lunch (sandwich or burger, fries, soda), no tip	$33.60
Afternoon break (soda and popcorn)	$14.35
Dinner at Italy (no alcoholic beverages) with tax & tip	$88
Souvenirs (Mickey T-shirts for Tim and Sandy) with tax*	$38.50
One-Day Total	$371.55
(does not include lodging or transportation)	
*Cheer up, you won't have to buy souvenirs every day.	

Babysitting

In the event that you want a little time away from your children, you have several options:

Evening Childcare Centers   Childcare isn't available within the theme parks, but each Magic Kingdom resort connected by the monorail and each Epcot resort (BoardWalk Inn and Villas, Yacht and Beach Club resorts) has a childcare center for toilet-trained children older than age three. Services vary, but children generally can be left between 4 p.m. and midnight. Milk and cookies and blankets and pillows are provided at all childcare centers. Play is supervised but not organized; toys, videos, and games are plentiful. Guests at any Disney resort or campground may use the childcare services.

The most elaborate of the childcare centers (variously called "clubs" or "camps") is Neverland Club at the Polynesian Resort. This and the one at the Wilderness Lodge are the only centers that include a buffet dinner at the club, though at the other locations you can arrange for room service to provide your children's meals. The rates for children ages 4 to 12 are $8 per hour for the first child and $6 per hour for each additional child.

We get a lot of mail praising the Neverland Club. A dad from Snohomish, Washington, writes:

> *The boys loved it! They got a good choice of food to eat in buffet style. It was educational—someone from Discovery Island brought some animals in—and it was fun. There was something for every age—appropriate toys, games, and a game room with free video games. The boys also had a Polaroid picture taken with Goofy, and the boys' smiles showed how good a time they were having. The supervisors seemed very pleasant and caring. As you might expect, it was all very professional and well done, and the beepers they had us carry made us feel extra secure.*

A Houston dad adds:

> *There were some outstanding surprises during our visit. One was the babysitting club at the Polynesian Hotel, the Neverland Club. I can tell you that our children enjoyed the Neverland Club as much as anything at WDW.*

If you're staying in a Disney resort that doesn't offer a child-care club and you don't have a car, you're better off using in-room babysitting. Trying to take your child to a club in another hotel via Disney bus requires a 50- to 90-minute trip each way. By the time you have deposited your little one, it will almost be time to pick him or her up again. Be aware that the childcare clubs shut down at or before midnight. If you intend to make a late night of it, in-room babysitting is your best bet.

Childcare Clubs*			
Hotel	**Program**	**Ages**	**Phone**
Wyndham Palace	All about Kids	All	(407) 827-2727
BoardWalk Inn & Villas	Harbor Club	4–12	(407) 939-5100
Contemporary Resort	Mouseketeer Clubhouse	4–12	(407) 824-1000
Grand Floridian Beach Resort	Mouseketeer Club	4–12	(407) 824-3000
The Hilton	Vacation Station	4–12	(407) 827-4000
Polynesian Resort	Neverland Club	4–12	(407) 824-2170
Wilderness Lodge Resort	Cub's Den	4–12	(407) 824-1083
Yacht and Beach Club	Sandcastle Club	4–12	(407) 934-7000

*Childcare clubs operate afternoons and evenings. All require reservations.

Day Care   Kinder-Care Learning Centers also operate childcare facilities at Walt Disney World. Originally developed for use by Disney employees, the centers now also take guests' children on a space-available basis. Kinder-Care provides basically the same services as a hotel club, except that the daytime *Learning While Playing Development Program* is more structured and educational. For childcare in the morning and early afternoon, Kinder-Care is the only game in town, but the service is closed on Saturdays and Sundays. Accepted are children ages 1 (provided they're walking and can eat table food) through 12. For reservations, call (407) 827-5437 or (407) 824-3290.

In-Room Babysitting   For those staying in the World, in-room babysitting is offered by Kinder-Care (phone (407) 827-5444) and the Fairy Godmothers (no kidding) service described below. Base rates for Kinder-Care are $11 an hour.

Outside Walt Disney World, childcare services and in-room babysitting can be arranged through most larger hotels and motels or by calling the Fairy Godmothers. Godmothers are on call 24 hours a day (you never get an answering machine) and offer the most flexible and diversified service in town. They will come to any hotel at any hour. If you pay, they will also take your children to the theme parks. No child is too young or too old, and Godmothers also care for the elderly and pets. All sitters are female nonsmokers. Base rates are $9 an hour for up to three children (in the same family), with a four-hour minimum and a $5 travel fee. For additional children in the same family, add $1 per child per hour. Godmothers will also tend a group of four or fewer children from different families for $6 an hour per family. For each additional child in excess of four, add $1 per child per hour to the base rate. Wishing won't get you a Godmother; you have to call (407) 277-3724 or (407) 275-7326.

WALT DISNEY WORLD LEARNING PROGRAMS FOR CHILDREN

Developed in coordination with leading educators and produced through the Disney Institute, Walt Disney World offers five programs for children 7–10, and six programs for children 11–15. Most programs last 3½ hours and are offered twice each week. Each course is $69 per child. Two courses taken on the same day cost $99 with lunch available for an additional charge. If the class visits a Disney theme park, admission is included. Due to small class sizes, you should make reservations six weeks in advance by calling (407) WDW-TOUR.

Disney is constantly tinkering with the learning programs. Some change and others are terminated to make room for new programs. Though the focus and presentation may vary, there are always programs available on art (including animation and architecture), performing arts (singing, dancing, acting, theatrical make-up, and backstage skills), and nature and ecology. Following are the specific courses offered when we went to press:

Programs For 7–10 Year Olds

Broadway Bound	Hands-on introduction to stage show skills at the Magic Kingdom and the Disney-MGM Studios.
Face Magic	Course on theatrical make-up (You won't recognize your child when you pick him up).
Art Surround	Kids tour theme parks to see how Disney artists translate concept into reality. Includes hands on project.
Kidventure	Excursion into the Florida wetlands by boat for wildlife identification and hands-on animal encounters.
Swamp Stomp	Exploration of a Florida cypress swamp followed by a trip to Epcot to learn about the "Circle of Life."

Programs For 11–15 Year Olds

Art Magic	Introduction to animation.
Showbiz Magic	Behind the scenes look at what goes into a theater attraction, including lighting, sound, Audio-Animatronics, and special effects.
Funny Papers	Participants learn how to create a story board and draw Disney characters.
Stealing the Show	Kids go through the Walt Disney World talent process from audition to putting it all together for a live show.
Rock Climbing for Youth	Introduction to rock climbing on an artificial climbing wall.
Island Explorers	Wildlife identification and specimen collecting field trip into a marsh. Micro scope, journals, and field-sketching techniques are covered.

Part Three

Where to Stay

When traveling with children your hotel is your home away from home, your safe harbor, and your sanctuary. Staying in a hotel, an activity usually reserved for adults, is in itself a great adventure for children. They take in every detail and delight in such things as having a pool at their disposal and obtaining ice from a noisy machine. Of course, it is critical that your children feel safe and secure, but it adds immeasurably to the success of the vacation if they really like the hotel.

In truth, because of their youth and limited experience, kids are far less particular about hotels than adults tend to be. A spartan room and a small pool at a budget motel will make most kids happier than a beagle with a lamb chop. But kids' memories are like little steel traps, so once you establish a lodging standard, that's pretty much what they'll expect every time. A couple from Gary, Indiana, stayed at the pricey Yacht Club Resort at Walt Disney World because they heard that it offered a knockout swimming area (true). When they returned two years later and stayed at Disney's All-Star Resort for about a third the price, their ten-year-old carped all week. If you're on a budget, it's better to begin with more modest accommodations and move up to better digs on subsequent trips as finances permit.

YOU CAN'T ROLLER SKATE IN A BUFFALO HERD

This was a song title from the 1960s. If we wrote that song today we'd call it, "You Can't Have Fun at Disney World if You're Drop-Dead Tired." Believe us, Walt Disney World is an easy place to be penny wise and pound foolish. Many families who cut lodging expense by booking a budget hotel end up so far away from Walt Disney World that it is a major hassle to return to the hotel in the middle of the day for swimming and a nap. By trying to spend the whole day at the theme parks, however, they wear themselves out quickly, and the dream vacation suddenly disintegrates into short tempers and exhaustion. In our opinion, if you are traveling with a child age 12 or younger, one of your top priorities should be to book a hotel within easy striking distance of the parks. For your sanity and enjoyment, and for the protection of your vacation investment, you absolutely must get your family some midday rest. And don't confuse this advice as a sales pitch for Disney hotels. There are, you will find, dozens of hotels outside Walt Disney World that are as close or closer to certain Disney theme parks than some of the resorts inside the World. Our main point—in fact, our only point—is to make it easy on yourself to return to your hotel when the need arises.

Some Basic Considerations

Cost

A night in a hotel at Disney World or the surrounding area can run anywhere from $30 to $500 a night. Clearly, if you are willing to sacrifice some luxury and don't mind a 10- to 25-minute commute, you can really cut your lodging costs by staying outside Walt Disney World. Hotels in Walt Disney World tend to be the most expensive, but they also offer some of the highest quality as well as a number of perks not enjoyed by guests who stay outside of Walt Disney World.

What It Costs to Stay in a Disney Resort Hotel	
Grand Floridian	$330–550
Polynesian Resort	$300–450
Swan (Westin)	$315–400
Dolphin (Sheraton)	$315–400
Beach Club Resort	$295–450
Yacht Club Resort	$295–450
BoardWalk Inn	$295–450

What It Costs to Stay in a Disney Resort Hotel (continued)	
BoardWalk Villas	$295–350 (studio)
Old Key West Resort	$250–290 (studio)
Contemporary Resort	$230–415
Villas at the Disney Institute	$225–265 (bungalow)
Wilderness Lodge	$220–340
Coronado Springs Resort	$130–160
Caribbean Beach Resort	$130–160
Dixie Landings Resort	$130–160
Port Orleans Resort	$130–160
All-Star resorts	$85–100

What It Costs to Stay in the Disney Village Hotel Plaza	
Wyndham Palace	$170–400
The Hilton Resort	$165–325
DoubleTree Guest Suites Resort	$150–475
Best Western Hotel	$125–300
Grosvenor Resort	$125–215
Hotel Royal Plaza	$115–250
Courtyard by Marriott	$115–190

LOCATION AND TRANSPORTATION OPTIONS

Once you have determined your budget, think about what you want to do at Walt Disney World. Will you go to all four theme parks, or will you concentrate on one or two? If you intend to use your own car, the location of your Disney hotel isn't especially important unless you plan to spend most of your time at the Magic Kingdom. (Disney transportation is always more efficient than your car in this case because it bypasses the Transportation and Ticket Center and deposits you right at the theme park entrance.)

Most convenient to the Magic Kingdom are the monorail hotels, the Grand Floridian, the Contemporary, and the Polynesian

Resorts. Linked by direct boat to the Magic Kingdom is the Wilderness Lodge.

Most convenient to Epcot and Disney-MGM Studios are the BoardWalk Inn, BoardWalk Villas, Yacht and Beach Club Resorts, and Swan and Dolphin. Though all are within easy walking distance of Epcot's International Gateway, boat service is also available. Vessels also connect Epcot hotels to Disney-MGM Studios. Epcot hotels are best for guests planning to spend most of their time at Epcot and/or Disney-MGM Studios. For the record, the resorts within walking distance of the International Gateway (the backdoor, so to speak) of Epcot are expensive and are a long, long walk from Future World, the section of Epcot where families tend to spend most of their time.

If you plan to use Disney transportation and intend to visit all four major parks and one or more of the swimming theme parks, book a centrally located resort with good transportation connections. The Epcot resorts and the Polynesian, Caribbean Beach, Old Key West, Dixie Landings, and Port Orleans resorts fit the bill.

Though not centrally located, the All-Star and Coronado Springs resorts have very good bus service to all Walt Disney World destinations and are closest to the new Animal Kingdom theme park. Independent hotels on US 192 near the entrance to Walt Disney World are also just a few minutes from the Animal Kingdom. Wilderness Lodge and Fort Wilderness Campground have the most convoluted and inconvenient transportation service of the Disney hotels. The Villas at the Disney Institute and the Old Key West Resort also are transportationally challenged, that is, buses run less frequently than at other Disney resorts.

Commuting to and from the Theme Parks

For Visitors Lodging inside Walt Disney World   With three important exceptions, the fastest way to commute from your hotel to the theme parks and back is in your own car. And although many Walt Disney World guests use the Disney Transportation System and appreciate not having to drive, in the final analysis, based on timed comparisons, it is almost always less time-consuming to drive. The exceptions are these: (1) commuting to the Magic Kingdom from the hotels on the monorail (Grand Floridian, Polynesian, and Contemporary Resorts); (2) commuting to the Magic Kingdom from any Disney hotel by bus or boat;

and (3) commuting to Epcot on the monorail from the Polynesian Resort via the Transportation and Ticket Center.

If you stay at the Polynesian Resort, you can catch a direct monorail to the Magic Kingdom, and by walking a hundred yards or so to the Transportation and Ticket Center, you can catch a direct monorail to Epcot. Located at the nexus of the monorail system, the Polynesian is indisputably the most convenient of all hotels. From either the Magic Kingdom or Epcot, you can return to your hotel quickly and easily whenever you desire. Sound good? It is, but it costs between $300 and $400 per night.

Second to the Polynesian in terms of convenience are the Grand Floridian and Contemporary Resorts, also on the Magic Kingdom monorail, but they cost as much or more as the Polynesian. Less expensive Disney hotels transport you to the Magic Kingdom by bus or boat. For reasons described below, this is more efficient than driving your own car.

Driving Time to the Theme Parks for Visitors Lodging outside Walt Disney World   For those staying outside Walt Disney World, we've calculated the approximate commuting time to the major theme parks' parking lots from several off-World lodging areas. Add a few minutes to our times to pay your parking fee and park. Once parked at the Transportation and Ticket Center (Magic Kingdom parking lot), it takes an average of 20 to 30 more minutes to reach the Magic Kingdom. To reach Epcot from its parking lot, add 7 to 10 minutes. At Disney-MGM Studios and the Animal Kingdom, the lot-to-gate transit is 5 to 10 minutes. If you haven't purchased your theme park admission in advance, tack on another 10 to 20 minutes.

Driving Time to the Theme Parks				
Minutes To: **Minutes From**	**Magic Kingdom Parking Lot**	**Epcot Parking Lot**	**Disney MGM Studios Parking Lot**	**Animal Kingdom Parking Lot**
Downtown Orlando	35	31	33	37
North International Dr. and Universal Studios	24	21	22	26
Central International Dr.—Sand Lake Road	26	23	24	27

Driving Time to the Theme Parks				
Minutes To: **Minutes From**	**Magic Kingdom Parking Lot**	**Epcot Parking Lot**	**Disney MGM Studios Parking Lot**	**Animal Kingdom Parking Lot**
South International Dr. and Sea World	18	15	16	20
FL 535	12	9	10	13
FL 192, north of I-4	10–15	7–12	5–10	5–10
FL 192, south of I-4	10–18	7–15	5–13	5–12

Shuttle Service from Hotels outside Walt Disney World
Many hotels in Walt Disney World area provide shuttle service to the theme parks. They represent a fairly carefree alternative for getting to and from the parks, letting you off near the entrance (except for the Magic Kingdom), and saving you the cost of parking. The rub is that they might not get you there as early as you desire (a critical point if you take our touring advice) or be available at the time you wish to return to your lodging. Also, be forewarned that most shuttle services do not add additional vehicles at park opening or closing times. In the morning your biggest problem is that you might not get a seat. At closing time, however, and sometimes following a hard rain, you can expect a lot of competition for space on the bus. If there's not room for everyone, you might have to wait 30 minutes to an hour for the next shuttle.

Convenience Conveniently Defined   Conceptually, it's easy to grasp that a hotel that is closer is more convenient than one that is far away. But nothing is that simple at Walt Disney World, so we'd better tell you exactly what you're in for. If you stay a Walt Disney World resort and use the Disney transportation system, you'll have a five- to ten-minute walk to the bus stop, monorail station, or dock (whichever applies). Once there, buses, trains, or boats generally run about every 15 to 20 minutes, so you might have to wait a short time for your transportation to arrive. Once on board, most conveyances make additional stops en route to your destination, and many take a less than direct route. Upon arrival, however, they deposit you fairly close to the entrance of the theme park. Returning to your hotel is the same process in reverse and takes about the same amount of time.

Regardless of whether you stay in a Walt Disney World or not, if you use your own car, here's how your commute shakes out. After a one- to five-minute walk from your room to your car, you drive to the theme park, stopping to pay a parking fee or showing your Disney ID for free parking (if you are a Disney resort guest). Disney cast members then direct you to a parking space. If you arrive early your space may be close enough to the park entrance (Magic Kingdom excepted) to walk. If you park farther afield, a Disney tram will come along every five minutes to collect you and transport you to the entrance.

At the Magic Kingdom, the entrance to the theme park is away-and-gone, separated from the parking lot by the Transportation and Ticket Center (TTC) and the Seven Seas Lagoon. After parking at the Magic Kingdom lot, you take a tram to the TTC and there board a ferry or monorail (your choice) for the trip across the lagoon to the theme park. All this is fairly time consuming and is to be avoided if possible. The only way to avoid it, however, is to lodge in a Disney hotel and commute directly to the Magic Kingdom entrance via Disney bus, boat, or monorail. Happily, all of the other theme parks are situated adjacent to their parking lot.

Because families with children tend to spend more time on average at the Magic Kingdom than at the other parks, and because it's so important to return to your hotel for rest, the business of getting around the lagoon can be a major consideration when choosing a place to stay. To cut to the essence, the extra hassle of crossing the lagoon (to get back to your car) makes coming and going much more difficult. The half hour it takes to commute to your hotel via car from the Animal Kingdom, Disney-MGM Studios, or Epcot takes an hour or longer from the Magic Kingdom. If you stay in a Disney hotel and use the Disney transportation system, you may have to wait five to ten minutes for your bus, boat, or monorail, but it will take you directly from the Magic Kingdom entrance to your hotel, bypassing the lagoon and the TTC.

DINING

Dining figures into the discussion of where to stay only if you don't plan to have a car at your disposal. If you have a car, you can go eat wherever you want. Alternatively, if you plan on using the Disney Transportation System (for Disney hotel guests) or the courtesy shuttle of your non-Disney hotel, you will either have to dine at the theme park or at or near your hotel. If your hotel offers a lot of choice or if there are other restaurants within walking distance, then there's no problem. If your hotel is somewhat isolated and offers limited selection, you'll feel like the people on a canoe trip the author once took who ate northern pike at every meal for a week because that's all they could catch.

At Walt Disney World, although it's relatively quick and efficient to commute from your Disney hotel or campground to the theme parks, it's a long, arduous process requiring transfers to travel from hotel to hotel. Disney hotels that are somewhat isolated and that offer limited dining choices include the Old Key West, Caribbean Beach, All-Star, Coronado Springs, and Wilderness Lodge Resorts as well as the Fort Wilderness Campground.

If you want a condo-type accommodation so that you have more flexibility for meal preparation than eating out of a cooler, the best deals in Walt Disney World are the Wilderness Homes (house trailers) and Cabins (prefab log cabins) at the Fort Wilderness Campground. Other Disney lodging with kitchens are available at the BoardWalk Villas, Old Key West, and the Disney Institute, but all are much more expensive than the homes and cabins at the campground. Outside Walt Disney World there are an ever-increasing number of condos available, and some are very good deals. See our discussion of lodging outside of Walt Disney World later in this chapter.

THE SIZE OF YOUR GROUP

Larger families and groups may be interested in how many people can be accommodated in a Disney resort room, but only Lilliputians would be comfortable in a room filled to capacity. Groups requiring two or more guest rooms should consider condo/suite/villa accommodations, either in or out of Walt Disney World. The most cost-efficient lodging in Walt Disney World for groups of five or six people are the cabins or the wilderness homes at Fort Wilderness Campground. Both sleep six adults plus a child or toddler in a crib. If there are more than six in your party, you will need either two hotel rooms, a suite (see Wilderness Lodge below), or a condo.

Hotel	Maximum Number of People per Room
All-Star resorts	4 people plus child in crib
Beach Club Resort	5 people plus child in crib
BoardWalk Inn	4 or 5 people plus child in crib
BoardWalk Villas	8 people plus child in crib
Caribbean Beach Resort	4 people plus child in crib
Contemporary Resort	5 people plus child in crib
Coronado Springs Resort	4 people plus child in crib
Dixie Landings Resort	4 people plus child in crib; 5 people in room with child's trundle bed
Dolphin (Sheraton)	4 people
Fort Wilderness Homes	6 people plus child in crib
Grand Floridian Beach Resort	4 or 5 people plus child in crib
Old Key West Resort	8 people plus child in crib
Polynesian Resort	5 people plus child in crib
Port Orleans Resort	4 people plus child in crib
Swan (Westin)	4 people
Villas at Disney Institute	8 people plus child in crib
Wilderness Lodge	4 people plus child in crib; junior suites with bunk beds accommodate 6 people
Yacht Club Resort	5 people plus child in crib

Sharing a Room with Your Children   If you share a room with your children, don't expect them to fall asleep while you've still got the lights and TV on. Generally speaking, you all need to hit the sack at the same time. We recommend establishing a single compromise bedtime, probably a little earlier than you like to go to bed and a bit later than the child's usual weekend bedtime. Observe any nightly rituals that you practice at home, such as reading a book before lights out.

STAYING IN OR OUT OF THE WORLD: WEIGHING THE PROS AND CONS

1. Cost   If cost is your primary consideration, you'll lodge much less expensively outside Walt Disney World.

2. Ease of Access   Even if you stay in Walt Disney World, you're dependent on some mode of transportation. It may be less stressful to use Disney transportation, but with the single exception of commuting to the Magic Kingdom, the fastest, most efficient, and most flexible way to get around usually is a car. If you're at Epcot, for example, and want to take the kids back to Disney's Grand Floridian Beach Resort for a nap, forget the monorail. You'll get back much faster in your own car.

A reader from Raynham, Massachusetts, who stayed at the Caribbean Beach Resort (and liked it very much) writes:

> *Even though the resort is on the Disney bus line, I recommend renting a car if it [fits] one's budget. The buses do not go directly to many destinations and often you have to switch at the Transportation and Ticket Center. Getting a [bus] seat in the morning is no problem [because] they allow standees. Getting a bus back to the hotel after a hard day can mean a long wait in line."*

It must be said that the Disney Transportation System is about as efficient as is humanly possible. No matter where you're going, you rarely wait more than 15 to 20 minutes for a bus, monorail, or boat. Although it is only for the use and benefit of Disney guests, nevertheless it is public transportation, and users must expect the inconveniences inherent in any transportation system: conveyances that arrive and depart on their schedule, not yours; the occasional need to transfer; multiple stops; time lost loading and unloading large numbers of passengers; and, generally, the challenge of understanding and using a large, complex transportation network.

3. Splitting Up   If you're in a party that probably will split up to tour (as frequently happens in families with children of widely varying ages), staying in the World offers more transportation options and, thus, more independence. Mom and Dad can take the car and return to the hotel for a relaxed dinner and early bedtime, while the teens remain in the park for evening parades and fireworks.

4. Slopping the Pigs   If you have a large crew that chows down like pigs at the trough, you may do better staying outside the World, where food is far less expensive.

5. Visiting Other Orlando-Area Attractions   If you plan to visit Sea World, Kennedy Space Center, the Universal theme parks, or other area attractions, it may be more convenient to stay outside the World. Don't, however, book a hotel halfway to Orlando because you think you might run over to Universal or Sea World for a day. Remember the Number One Rule: "Stay close enough to Walt Disney World to return to your hotel for rest in the middle of the day."

Walt Disney World Lodging

BENEFITS OF STAYING IN WALT DISNEY WORLD

In addition to proximity—especially easy access to the Magic Kingdom—Walt Disney World resort hotel and campground guests are accorded other privileges and amenities unavailable to those staying outside the World. Though some of these perks are only advertising gimmicks, others are potentially quite valuable. Here are the benefits and what they mean:

1. Early Entry at the Theme Parks   Walt Disney World lodging guests (excluding guests at the independent hotels of Disney Village Hotel Plaza) are invited to enter a designated theme park one hour earlier than the general public each day. Disney lodging guests are also offered specials on admission, including a passport good for the exact number of days of their visit and discount tickets to the water theme parks. These benefits are subject to change without notice. The early-entry program, however, is well established.

Early entry can be quite valuable during peak season, when the parks are mobbed. If you're willing to get up before sunrise and arrive at the park as early as 6:30 a.m., you'll be rewarded with the least congested, most stress-free touring of your vacation. Early entry is also handy in the off-season, when the parks often close early. Though crowds are manageable at these times, adding an extra hour and a half to an otherwise short touring day significantly increases the number of attractions you'll be able to see.

2. Themed Hotels   All of the Disney hotels are themed, in pointed contrast to non-Disney hotels, which are, well, mostly just hotels. Each Disney hotel is designed to make you feel you're in a special place or period of history. Here are the themes at Disney resorts:

Hotel	Theme
All-Star resorts	Sports and music
Beach Club Resort	New England beach club of the 1870s
BoardWalk Inn	East Coast boardwalk hotel of the early 1900s
BoardWalk Villas	East Coast beach cottage of the early 1900s
Caribbean Beach Resort	Caribbean islands
Contemporary Resort	The future as perceived by past and present generations
Coronado Springs Resort	Northern Mexico and the American Southwest
Dixie Landings Resort	Life on the Mississippi in the antebellum South
Dolphin (Sheraton)	Modern Florida resort
Grand Floridian Beach Resort	Turn-of-the-century luxury hotel
Old Key West Resort	Key West
Polynesian Resort	Hawaii/South Sea islands
Port Orleans	Turn-of-the-century New Orleans and Mardi Gras
Swan (Westin)	Modern Florida resort
Villas at the Disney Institute	Combination rustic villas and country club atmosphere
Wilderness Lodge	National park grand lodge of the early 1900s in the American Northwest
Yacht Club Resort	New England seashore hotel of the 1880s

Theming is a huge attraction for children, firing their imaginations, and really making the hotel an adventure and a memorable place to be. Some resorts carry off their themes better than others, and some themes are more exciting. The Wilderness Lodge, for example, is extraordinary. The lobby opens eight stories to a timbered ceiling supported by giant columns of bundled logs. One look eases you into the Northwest wilderness theme. Romantic and isolated, the lodge is heaven for children.

The Polynesian, also dramatic, conveys the feeling of the Pacific islands. It's great for families. Waterfront rooms in the Moorea building offer a perfect view of the Cinderella Castle and the Magic Kingdom fireworks across Seven Seas Lagoon. Kids don't know Polynesia from amnesia, but they like those cool "lodge" buildings and all the torches at night.

Grandeur, nostalgia, and privilege are central to the Grand Floridian and Yacht and Beach Club resorts and the BoardWalk Inn and Villas. Although modeled after eastern seaboard hotels of different eras, the resorts are amazingly similar. Thematic distinctions are subtle and are lost on many guests. Children appreciate the creative swimming facilities of these resorts, but are relatively neutral toward the themes.

The Port Orleans Resort lacks the real mystery and sultriness of the New Orleans French Quarter, but it's hard to replicate the Big Easy in a sanitized Disney version. Dixie Landings, however, hits the mark with its antebellum Mississippi River theme, as does Old Key West Resort with its Florida Keys theme. The Caribbean Beach Resort's theme is much more effective at night, thanks to creative lighting. By day, the resort looks like a Miami condo development. Children like all four of these resorts, even though the themes are a bit removed from their frame of reference. All four resorts are more spread out and the buildings built to a more human (two- or three-story) scale.

Coronado Springs Resort offers several styles of Mexican and Southwestern American architecture. Though the lake setting is lovely and the resort is attractive and inviting, the theme (with the exception of the main swimming area) isn't particularly stimulating. Coronado Springs feels more like a Scottsdale, Arizona, country club than a Disney resort.

The All-Star Resort encompasses 30 three-story, T-shaped hotels with almost 6,000 guest rooms. There are 15 themed areas: five celebrate sports (surfing, basketball, tennis, football, and baseball), five recall Hollywood movie themes, and five have musical motifs. The resort's design, with entrances shaped like musical notes, Coke cups, and footballs, is somewhat adolescent, sacrificing grace and beauty for energy and novelty. Guest rooms are small, with decor reminiscent of a teenage boy's bedroom. Despite the theme, there are no sports, movies, or music at the All-Star Sports Resort. For children, staying at the All-Star resorts is like being a permanent resident at a miniature golf course: They can't get enough of the giant footballs, Dalmatians, and guitars. On a more subjective level, kids intuit that the All-Star resorts are pretty close to what you'd get all the time if Disney had 12-year-olds designing their hotels. It's cool, and they feel right at home.

Pretense aside, the Contemporary, Swan, and Dolphin are essentially themeless, but architecturally interesting. The Contemporary is a 15-story, A-frame building with monorails running through the middle. Views from guest rooms in the Contemporary Tower are among the best at Walt Disney World. The Swan and Dolphin resorts are massive, yet whimsical. Designed by Michael Graves, they're excellent examples of "entertainment architecture." Unfortunately, a little too much whimsy and entertainment worked their way into the guest rooms, which are "busy," bordering on garish. Children are blown away by the giant fish and swans atop the Dolphin and Swan and love the idea of the monorail running through the middle of the Contemporary.

3. Great Swimming Areas   Walt Disney World resorts offer some of the most imaginative swimming facilities that you are likely to encounter anywhere. Exotically themed, beautifully landscaped, and equipped with slides, fountains, and smaller pools for toddlers, Disney resort swimming complexes are a quantum leap removed from the typical, rectangular, hotel swimming pool. Some resorts, like the Grand Floridian and the Polynesian, even offer a sand beach on the Seven Seas Lagoon in addition to swimming pools. Others, like the Caribbean Beach and Dixie Landings Resorts, have provided elaborate themed playgrounds near their swimming areas. Incidentally, lest there be any confusion, we are talking about Disney hotel swimming areas and not the Disney paid-admission water theme parks (River Country, Typhoon Lagoon, and Blizzard Beach).

4. Babysitting and Childcare Options A number of options for baby-sitting, childcare, and children's programs are offered to Disney hotel and campground guests. Each of the resort hotels connected by the monorail, as well as several other Disney hotels, offers "clubs," or themed childcare centers, where potty-trained children ages 3 to 12 can stay while the adults go out.

Though somewhat expensive, the clubs do a great job and are highly regarded by children and parents. On the negative side, they're open only in the evening and not all Disney hotels have them. If you're staying at a Disney hotel that doesn't have a child-care club, you're better off using one of the private in-room babysitting services such as Fairy Godmother or Kinder-Care (see page 50). In-room babysitting is also available at hotels outside Walt Disney World.

5. Guaranteed Theme Park Admissions On days of unusually heavy attendance, Disney resort guests are guaranteed admission to the theme parks. In practice, no guest is ever turned away until a theme park's parking lot is full. When this happens, that park most certainly will be packed to the point of absolute gridlock. Under such conditions, you would have to possess the common sense of an amoeba to exercise your guaranteed-admission privilege. The privilege, by the way, doesn't extend to the swimming parks, Blizzard Beach, Typhoon Lagoon, and River Country.

6. Children Sharing a Room with Their Parents There is no extra charge per night for children younger than age 18 sharing a room with their parents. Many hotels outside Walt Disney World also observe this practice.

7. Free Parking Disney resort guests with cars don't have to pay for parking in the theme park lots. This privilege saves about $6 per day.

8. Free Purchase Delivery Disney resort guests can have their Walt Disney World purchases delivered to their hotel rooms for free, saving them the hassle of lugging extra items around or waiting in lines at crowded Package Pickup Centers.

How to Get Discounts on Lodging at Walt Disney World

There are so many guest rooms in and around Walt Disney World that competition is brisk, and everyone, including Disney, wheels and deals to keep them filled. This has led to a more flexible discount policy for Walt Disney World hotels. Here are tips for getting price breaks:

1. Seasonal Savings   You can save $15–50 per night on a Walt Disney World hotel room by scheduling your visit during the slower times of the year.

2. Ask about Specials   When you talk to Disney reservationists, inquire specifically about special deals. Ask, for example, "What special rates or discounts are available at Disney hotels during the time of our visit?"

3. Ocala Disney AAA Travel Center   The Ocala Disney AAA Travel Center off I-75 in Ocala, Florida, routinely books Disney hotel rooms at discounts of up to 43%! Because the program is designed to snare uncommitted travelers, you must reserve your room in person at the center. If you call in advance and tell staffers you're on your way down, however, they usually will tell you what's available and at what discount. The phone number is (352) 854-0770. You can also arrange priority seating for dining. The center is open from 9 a.m. to 6 p.m. daily.

4. Travel Agents   Travel agents are particularly good sources of information on time-limited special programs and discounts.

5. Magic Kingdom Club Gold Card   Good for discounts on rooms, theme park admission, and shopping. You also get a subscription to the Disney magazine. Persons not signed up through work (as an employee benefit) can buy a 2-year individual Magic Kingdom Club Gold Card for about $65. A seniors card is about $50. For information, call (714) 781-1550 or write:

Magic Kingdom Club Gold Card
P.O. Box 3850
Anaheim, CA 92803-9832

A dad from Bay Minette, Alabama, chastised us for not giving the Gold Card its due:

You didn't say much about the MK Club Gold Card. We went again in late September. It was really crowded. We bought the MK Club Gold Card and saved $300–400 on our rooms and tickets.

6. Organizations and Auto Clubs   Eager to sell rooms, Disney has developed time-limited programs with some auto clubs and other organizations. Recently, for example, AAA members were offered a 10–20% savings on Disney hotels, preferred parking at the theme parks, and discounts on Disney package vacations. Such deals come and go, but the market suggests there will be more in the next year. If you're a member of AARP, AAA, or any travel or auto club, ask whether the group has a program before shopping elsewhere.

A WORD ABOUT CAMPING AT WALT DISNEY WORLD

Fort Wilderness Campground is a spacious resort campground for tent and RV camping. Fully equipped, air-conditioned trailers also are available for rent, as are newer prefab log cabins. The log cabins offer essentially the same square footage as the trailers (known as "wilderness homes"), but are newer, more aesthetically appealing and have an elevated outdoor deck. Campsites, "preferred" or "regular," are arranged on loops branching from three thoroughfares. The only difference between a preferred and regular campsite is that preferred sites are closer to the campground amenities (swimming pools, restaurants, and shopping). Each site has a 110- and 220-volt outlet, picnic table, and grill. Most RV sites have sanitary hook-ups. RV sites are roomy by eastern U.S. standards, but tent campers will probably feel a little cramped. On any day, about 90% of campers will be RVers.

When booking, tent campers should request a site on Loop 1500, Cottontail Curl, or on Loop 2000, Spanish Moss Lane. The better loops for RVers are Loops 200, 400, 500, and 1400. All loops have a comfort station with showers, toilets, phones, an ice machine, and a coin laundry.

Rental trailers and cabins offer a double bed and two bunk beds in the only bedroom, augmented by a Murphy bed (pulls down from the wall) in the living room. There is one rather small bathroom with shower and tub.

Aside from offering economy accommodations, Fort Wilderness Campground has a group camping area, evening entertainment, horseback riding, bike trails, jogging trails, swimming, and a petting farm. River Country water theme park is nearby. Access to the Magic Kingdom and Discovery Island is by boat from the Fort Wilderness landing on Bay Lake. Access to other destinations is by private car or shuttle bus.

If you rent a cabin or a wilderness home, particularly in the fall or spring, keep abreast of local weather conditions. These accommodations are essentially mobile homes, definitely not the place you want to be if the area is under a tornado warning.

Fort Wilderness Campground

784 campsites	boat/bus service	$35–68 per night
408 wilderness homes and cabins (sleeps 4–6)	boat/bus service	$185–230 per night

Lodging outside Walt Disney World

At this point you're probably wondering how, as mentioned above, a hotel outside Walt Disney World could be as convenient as one inside Walt Disney World? Well, Mable, Walt Disney World is a *muy largo* place, but like any city or state, it has borders. By way of analogy, let's say you want to stay in a hotel in Cincinnati, Ohio, but can't find one you can afford. Would you rather book a hotel in Toledo or Cleveland, which are both still in Ohio but pretty darn far away, or would you be willing to leave Ohio and stay just across the state line in Covington, Kentucky?

Just west of Walt Disney World on US 192 are a bunch of hotels and condos, some great bargains, that are closer to the Animal Kingdom and the Disney-MGM Studios than are many hotels in Walt Disney World. Similarly, there are hotels along Disney's east border, FL 535, that are exceptionally convenient if you plan to use your own car.

Lodging costs outside Walt Disney World vary incredibly. If you shop around, you can find a clean motel with a pool within 20 minutes of the World for as low as $35 a night. You also can find luxurious, expensive hotels with all the extras. Because of hot competition, discounts abound, particularly for AAA and AARP members.

Hotel Concentrations Around Orlando.

Lake Apopka

Winter Garden

Pine Hills

10

75

95

Orlando

95

17
92

Winter Park

50

Florida Turnpike

435

50

408

Orlando

4

527

Conway

436

Lake Butler

535

441

92

L. Tibet

482

L. Conway

Walt Disney World

2

528

Orlando International Airport

Vineland

L. Buena Vista

535

Internatl. Dr.

1

Orange Blossom Trail

Florida Turnpike

Ctl. Florida Greenway

417

192

27

4

536

Osceola Pkwy.

3

East Lake Tohopekaliga

417

192

Kissimmee

192

There are three primary out-of-the-World areas to consider:

1. International Drive Area   This area, about 15 to 20 minutes east of Walt Disney World, parallels I-4 on its southern side and offers a wide selection of both hotels and restaurants. Accommodations range from $35 to $250 per night. The chief drawbacks of the International Drive area are its terribly congested roads, countless traffic signals, and inadequate access to westbound I-4. More important, however, is that it just a bit too far away to return to your hotel for midday rest.

Hotels in the International Drive area are listed in the *Orlando Official Accommodations Guide* published by the Orlando/Orange County Convention and Visitors Bureau. For a copy, call (800) 255-5786 or (407) 363-5874.

2. Lake Buena Vista and the I-4 Corridor   A number of hotels are situated along FL 535 and north of I-4 between Walt Disney World and I-4's intersection with the Florida Turnpike. These properties are easily reached from the interstate and are near a large number of restaurants, including those on International Drive. Driving time to Disney World is 5 to 15 minutes. Most hotels in this area are listed in the *Orlando Official Accommodations Guide.*

3. US 192   This is the highway to Kissimmee, southeast of Walt Disney World. In addition to a number of large, full-service hotels are many small, privately owned motels that are a good value. Several dozen properties on US 192 are closer to the Disney theme parks than the more expensive hotels in Walt Disney World Village and the Disney Village Hotel Plaza. Traffic on US 192 is extremely heavy but usually moves smoothly. The number and variety of restaurants on US 192 has increased markedly in the past year, easing the area's primary shortcoming.

Hotels on US 192 and in Kissimmee are listed in the *Kissimmee–St. Cloud Tour & Travel Sales Guide,* available by calling (800) 327-9159.

CONDOMINIUMS AND SUITE HOTELS

A large number suite hotels and condo resorts in the Kissimmee/Orlando area rent to vacationers for a week or less. Look for bargains, especially during off-peak periods. Reservations and information can be obtained from:

Condolink	(800) 733-4445
Holiday Villas	(800) 251-1112
Hospitality Vacation Homes	(800) 969-7077
Kissimmee–St. Cloud Reservations	(800) 333-5477
Vistana Resort	(800) 877-8787
Ramada Suites by Sea World	(800) 633-1405
Holiday Inn Family Suites	(877) 387-KIDS

We frequently receive letters from readers extolling the virtues of renting a suite, condo, or vacation home. This endorsement by a family from Glenmont, New York, is typical:

> *I would recommend that you include the Vistana Resort in your hotel section. Such luxury for so little. On two past visits we stayed in Disney's Lake Buena Vista Hotel Village. To have two BR, two baths, kitchen, DR, LR, deck, and Jacuzzi for less money was heaven. The children could go to bed at 8:30, and we could stay up and have some privacy. The full kitchen saved $, too—especially at breakfast time. I highly recommend this for families. So close (five minutes to Epcot, ten to MK, seven to Sea World) and convenient.*

A majority of rental condos are listed with travel agents. Condo owners often pay an enhanced commission to agents who rent the units for reduced consumer rates.

GETTING A GOOD DEAL ON A ROOM OUTSIDE WALT DISNEY WORLD

Hotel development at Walt Disney World has sharpened the competition among lodgings throughout the Walt Disney World/Orlando/Kissimmee area. Hotels outside the World, in particular, struggle to fill their guest rooms. Unable to compete with Disney resorts for convenience or perks, off-World hotels lure patrons in with bargain rates. The extent of the bargain depends on the season, day of the week, and local events. Here are tips and strategies for getting a good deal on a room outside Walt Disney World.

1. Orlando MagiCard   Orlando MagiCard is a discount program sponsored by the Orlando/Orange County Convention and Visitors Bureau. Cardholders are eligible for discounts of 10% to 40% at approximately 75 participating hotels. The MagiCard is also good for discounts at area attractions, including Sea World, Cypress Gardens, Universal Studios, several dinner theaters, Church Street Station, and Disney's Pleasure Island. Valid for up to six people, the card isn't available for groups or conventions.

To obtain an Orlando MagiCard and a list of participating hotels and attractions, call (800) 255-5786 or (407) 363-5874. Anyone older than age 18 is eligible, and the card is free. If you miss getting a card before you leave home, you can get one at the Convention and Visitors Bureau at 8445 International Drive in Orlando. When you call for a MagiCard, also request the *Orlando Official Accommodations Guide* and the Orlando Vacation Planner.

2. Exit Information Guide   Exit Information Guide publishes a book of discount coupons for bargain rates at hotels statewide. The book is free in many restaurants and motels on main highways leading to Florida. Because most travelers make reservations before leaving home, picking up the coupon book en route doesn't help much. If you call and use a credit card, EIG will send the guide first class for $3 ($5 U.S. for Canadian delivery). Contact:

Exit Information Guide
4205 NW 6th Street
Gainesville, FL 32609
(352) 371-3948

3. Wholesalers, Consolidators, and Reservation Services Wholesalers and consolidators buy rooms, or options on rooms (room blocks), from hotels at a low, negotiated rate. They then resell the rooms at a profit through travel agents and tour packagers, or directly to the public. Wholesalers and consolidators often offer rooms at rates from 15 to 50% off rack rate, occasionally sacrificing profit to avoid returning the rooms unsold.

When wholesalers and consolidators deal directly with the public, they frequently represent themselves as "reservation services." When you call, ask for a rate for your chosen hotel or for the best deal in the area where you'd like to stay. State if there's a maximum amount you're willing to pay. The service likely will find something for you, even if it has to shave off a dollar or two of profit. You may have to pay by credit card when you reserve a room. Other times, you pay when you check out. Here are two services that frequently offer substantial discounts:

Accommodations Express	(800) 444-7666
Hotel Reservations Network	(800) 964-6835

4. Hotel Shopping on the Internet To read the popular press, you'd think hotels were giving rooms away on the Internet. While they're not, of course, it is true that hotels are increasingly using the Internet to fill rooms during slow periods and to advertise time-limited specials. The Internet is a communications tool, one of many in the hotel's toolbox, and they use it along with more traditional practices such as promoting specials through travel agents. If you enjoy cyber shopping, by all means have at it, but hotel shopping on the Internet is not nearly as quick or convenient as handing the task to your travel agent. And, get this: you'll be hard pressed to find a deal that is not also available through your agent. When we bump into a great deal on the Web, the first thing we do is to call our travel agent. Often our agent can beat the deal or improve on it (as in the case of an upgrade). Although a good travel agent working on his/her own can achieve great things, the same agent working with a savvy, helpful client can work wonders.

5. If You Make Your Own Reservation Always call the hotel in question, not the hotel chain's national 800 number. Often, reservationists at the toll-free number are unaware of local specials. Always ask about specials before you inquire about corporate rates. Don't hesitate to bargain, but do it before you check in. If you're buying a hotel's weekend package, for example, and want to extend your stay, you can often obtain at least the corporate rate for the extra days.

OUT-OF-THE-WORLD CHILDREN'S PROGRAMS

Many large non-Disney hotels offer supervised programs for children, some complimentary, some with fees. If you decide to take advantage of the kids' programs, call ahead to find out about specific children's events that are scheduled during your vacation. Ask about cost and the ages that can participate; the best programs divide children into age groups. Make reservations for activities your child might want to participate in. You can always cancel after arrival.

After checking in, visit with the kids' program staff. Ask about counselor-child ratio and whether the counselors are trained in first aid and CPR. Briefly introduce your children to the staff and setting, which typically will leave them wanting more, thereby easing the separation anxiety when they return to stay.

How to Childproof a Hotel Room

Toddlers and small children up to three years of age (and sometimes older) can wreak mayhem if not outright disaster in a hotel room. They're mobile, curious, and amazingly fast, and they have a penchant for turning the most seemingly innocuous furnishing or decoration into a lethal weapon. Chances are you're pretty experienced when it comes to spotting potential dangers, but just in case you need a refresher course, here's what to look for.

Always begin by checking the room for hazards that you cannot neutralize, like balconies, chipping paint, cracked walls, sharp surfaces, shag carpeting, and windows that can't be secured shut. If you encounter anything that you don't like or is too much of a hassle to fix, ask for another room.

If you use a crib supplied by the hotel, make sure that the mattress is firm and covers the entire bottom of the crib. If there is a mattress cover, it should fit tightly. Slats should be $2\frac{3}{8}$ inch or less apart. Test the drop sides to ensure that they work properly and that your child cannot release them accidentally. Examine the crib from all angles (including from underneath) to make sure it has been assembled correctly and that there are no sharp edges. Check for chipping paint and other potentially toxic substances that you child might ingest. Wipe down surfaces your child might touch or mouth to diminish the potential of infection transmitted from a previous occupant. Finally, position the crib away from drape cords, heaters, wall sockets, and air conditioners.

If your infant can turn over, we recommend changing him or her on a pad on the floor. Likewise, if you have a child seat of any sort, place it where it cannot be knocked over, and always strap your child in.

If your child can roll, crawl, or walk you should bring about eight electrical outlet covers and some cord to tie cabinets shut and to bind drape cords and the like out of reach. Check for appliances, lamps, ashtrays, ice buckets, and anything else that your child might pull down on him- or herself. Have the hotel remove coffee tables with sharp edges, and both real and artificial plants that are within your child's reach. Round up items from table and counter tops such as matchbooks, courtesy toiletries, and drinking glasses and store them out of reach.

If the bathroom door can be accidentally locked, cover the locking mechanism with duct tape or a doorknob cover. Use the security chain or upper latch on the room's entrance door to ensure that your child doesn't open it without your knowledge.

Inspect the floor and remove pins, coins, and other foreign objects that your child might find. Don't forget to check under beds and furniture. One of the best tips we've heard came from a Fort Lauderdale, Florida, mother who crawls around the room on her hands and knees in order to see possible hazards from her child's perspective.

If you rent a suite or a condo you'll have more territory to childproof and will have to deal with the possible presence of cleaning supplies, a stove, a refrigerator, cooking utensils, and low cabinet doors, among other things. Sometimes the best option is to seal off the kitchen with a folding safety gate.

Part Four

Disney Boot Camp: Basic Training for World-Bound Families

The Brutal Truth about Family Vacations

It has been suggested that the phrase *family vacation* is a bit of an oxymoron. This is because you can never take a vacation from the responsibilities of parenting if your children are traveling with you. Though you leave work and normal routine far behind, your children require as much attention, if not more, when traveling than at home.

Parenting on the road is an art. It requires imagination and organization. Think about it, you have to do all the usual stuff (feed, dress, bathe, supervise, teach, comfort, discipline, put to bed, and so on) in an atmosphere where your children are hyper-stimulated, and without the familiarity of place and the resources you take for granted at home. Although it's not impossible—and can even be fun—parenting on the road is not something you want to learn on the fly, particularly at Walt Disney World.

The point we want to drive home is that preparation, or the lack thereof, will make or break your Walt Disney World vacation. Believe us, you do *not* want to leave the success of your expensive Disney vacation to chance. But don't confuse chance with good luck. Chance is what happens when you fail to prepare. Good luck is when preparation meets opportunity.

Your preparation can be organized into several categories, all of which we will help you undertake. Broadly speaking, you need to prepare yourself and your children mentally, emotionally, physically, organizationally, and logistically. You also need a basic understanding of Walt Disney World and a well-considered plan for how to go about seeing it.

Mental and Emotional Preparation

This is a subject that we will touch on here and return to many times in this book. Mental preparation begins with realistic expectations about your Disney vacation and consideration of what each adult and child in your party most wants and needs from their Walt Disney World experience. Getting in touch with this aspect of planning requires a lot of introspection and good, open family communication.

DIVISION OF LABOR

Talk about what you and your partner need and what you expect to happen on the vacation. This discussion alone can preempt some unpleasant surprises midtrip. If you are a two-parent (or two-adult) family, do you have a clear understanding of how the parenting workload is to be distributed? We have seen some distinctly disruptive misunderstandings in two-parent households where one parent is (pardon the legalese) the primary caregiver. Often, the other parent expects the primary caregiver to function on vacation as she (or he) does at home. The primary caregiver, on the other hand, is ready for a break. She expects her partner to either shoulder the load equally or perhaps even assume the lion's share so she can have a *real* vacation. However you divide the responsibility, of course, is up to you. Just make sure you negotiate a clear understanding *before* you leave home.

TOGETHERNESS

Another dimension to consider is how much "togetherness" seems appropriate to you. For some parents, a vacation represents a rare opportunity to really connect with their children, to talk, exchange ideas, and get reacquainted. For others, a vacation affords the time to get a little distance, to enjoy a round of golf while the kids are participating in a program organized by the resort.

At Walt Disney World you can orchestrate your vacation to spend as much or as little time with your children as you desire, but more about that later. The point here is to think about your and your children's preferences and needs concerning your time together. A typical day at a Disney theme park provides the structure of experiencing attractions together, punctuated by periods of waiting in line, eating, and so on, which facilitate conversation and sharing. Most attractions can be enjoyed together by the whole family, regardless of age ranges. This allows for more congruence and less dissent when it comes to deciding what to see and do. For many parents and children, however, the rhythms of a Walt Disney World day seem to consist of passive entertainment experiences alternated with endless discussions of where to go and what to do next. As a mother from Winston-Salem, North Carolina, reported, "Our family mostly talked about what to do next with very little sharing or discussion about what we had seen. [The conversation] was pretty task oriented."

Two observations: First, fighting the crowds and keeping the family moving along can easily escalate into a pressure-driven outing. Having an advance plan or itinerary eliminates moment-to-moment guesswork and spontaneous decision making, thus creating more time for savoring and connecting. Second, external variables such as crowd size, noise, and heat, among others, can be so distracting as to preclude any meaningful togetherness. These negative impacts can be moderated, as we will discuss later, by your being selective concerning the time of year, day of the week, and time of day you visit the theme parks. The bottom line is that you can achieve the degree of connection and togetherness you desire with a little advance planning and a realistic awareness of the distractions you will encounter.

LIGHTEN UP

Prepare yourself mentally to be a little less compulsive on vacation about correcting small behavioral deviations and pounding home the lessons of life. Certainly, little Mildred will have to learn eventually that it's very un-Disney-like to take off her top at the pool. But there's plenty of time for that later. So what if Matt eats hamburgers for breakfast, lunch, and dinner every day? You can make him eat peas and broccoli when you get home and are in charge of the menu again. Roll with the little stuff, and remember when your children act out that they are wired to the max. At least some of that adrenaline is bound to spill out in undesirable ways. Coming down hard will send an already frayed little nervous system into orbit.

SOMETHING FOR EVERYONE

If you travel with an infant, toddler, or any child that requires a lot of special attention, make sure that you have some energy and time remaining for your other children. Try to schedule some time alone with each of your children, if not each day, then at least a couple of times during the trip. In the course of your planning, invite each child to name something special to do or see at Walt Disney World with mom or dad alone. Work these special activities into your trip itinerary. Whatever else, if you commit, write it down so that you don't forget. Remember, a casually expressed willingness to do this or that may be perceived as a promise by your children.

WHOSE IDEA WAS THIS ANYWAY?

A major discord that many families experience arises from the kids being on a completely different wavelength from mom and dad. Parents and grandparents are often worse than children are when it comes to conjuring up fantasy scenarios of what a Walt Disney World vacation will be like. A Disney vacation can be many things, but believe us when we tell you that there's a lot more to it than just riding Dumbo and seeing Mickey.

In our experience, most parents and nearly all grandparents expect children to enter a state of rapture at Walt Disney World, bouncing from attraction to attraction in wide-eyed wonder, appreciative beyond words to their adult benefactors. What they get, more often than not, is not even in the same ballpark. Preschoolers will, without a doubt, be wide-eyed, but less with delight than a general sense of being overwhelmed by noise, crowds, and Disney characters as big as tool sheds. We have substantiated through thousands of interviews and surveys that the best part of a Disney vacation for a preschooler is the hotel swimming pool. With grade schoolers and pre-driving-age teens you get near manic hyperactivity coupled with periods of studied nonchalance. This last, which relates to the importance of being "cool," translates into a maddening display of boredom and a "been there, done that" attitude. Older teens are the exponential version of the younger teens and grade schoolers, except without the manic behavior.

As a function of probability, you may escape some—but probably not all—of the above-described behaviors. Even in the event that they are all visited on you, however, take heart, there are antidotes.

For preschoolers you can keep things light and happy by limiting the time you spend in the theme parks. Short forays to the parks interspersed with naps, swimming, and quiet activities such as reading to your children will go a long way toward keeping things on an even keel. The most critical point is that the overstimulation of the parks must be balanced by adequate rest and more mellow activities. For grade schoolers and early teens, you can moderate the hyperactivity and false apathy by enlisting their help in planning the vacation, especially by allowing them to take a leading role in determining the itinerary for days at the theme parks. Being in charge of specific responsibilities that focus on the happiness of other family members also work well. One reader, for example, turned a 12-year-old liability into an asset by asking him to help guard against attractions that might frighten his 5-year-old sister.

Generally speaking, the more information your children have before arriving at Walt Disney World, the less likely they will be to act out. Knowledge enhances anticipation and at the same time affords a level of comfort and control that helps kids understand the big picture. The more they feel in control, the less they will act out of control.

DISNEY, KIDS, AND SCARY STUFF

Disney attractions, both rides and shows, are adventures. They focus on themes of all adventures: good and evil, death, beauty and the grotesque, fellowship and enmity. As you sample the attractions at Walt Disney World, you transcend the spinning and bouncing of midway rides to thought-provoking and emotionally powerful entertainment. All of the endings (except *Alien Encounter*) are happy, but the adventures' impact, given Disney's gift for special effects, often intimidates and occasionally frightens young children.

There are rides with menacing witches, burning towns, and ghouls popping out of their graves, all done with a sense of humor, provided you're old enough to understand the joke. And bones. There are bones everywhere: human bones, cattle bones, dinosaur bones, even whole skeletons. There's a stack of skulls at the headhunter's camp on the Jungle Cruise, a platoon of skeletons sailing ghost ships in Pirates of the Caribbean, and a haunting assemblage of skulls and skeletons in The Haunted Mansion. Skulls, skeletons, and bones punctuate Snow White's Adventures, Peter Pan's Flight, and Big Thunder Mountain Railroad. In the Animal Kingdom, there's an entire children's playground made up exclusively of giant bones and skeletons.

Monsters and special effects at Disney-MGM Studios are more real and sinister than those in the other theme parks. If your child has difficulty coping with the witch in Snow White's Adventures, think twice about exposing him or her to machine-gun battles, earthquakes, and the creature from *Alien* at the Studios.

One reader tells of taking his preschool children on Star Tours:

> *We took a four-year-old and a five-year-old, and they had the shit scared out of them at Star Tours. We did this first thing in the morning, and it took hours of Tom Sawyer Island and Small World to get back to normal.*
>
> *Our kids were the youngest by far in Star Tours. I assume that other adults had more sense or were not such avid readers of your book. Preschoolers should start with Dumbo and work up to the Jungle Cruise in late morning, after being revved up and before getting hungry, thirsty, or tired. Pirates of the Caribbean is out for preschoolers. You get the idea.*

At Walt Disney World, anticipate the almost inevitable emotional overload as your young children struggle to cope. Be sensitive, alert, and prepared for practically anything, even behavior that is out of character for your child at home. Most young children take Disney's macabre trappings in stride, and others are easily comforted by an arm around the shoulder or a squeeze of the hand. Parents who know that their children tend to become upset should take it slow and easy, sampling more benign adventures, gauging reactions, and discussing with the children how they felt about what they saw.

Some Tips

1. Start Slow and Warm Up   While each major theme park offers several fairly unintimidating attractions that you can sample to determine your child's relative sensitivity, the Magic Kingdom is probably the best testing ground. At the Magic Kingdom try Buzz Lightyear's Space Ranger Spin in Tomorrowland, Peter Pan in Fantasyland, and the Jungle Cruise in Adventureland to measure your child's reaction to unfamiliar sights and sounds. If your child takes these in stride, try Pirates of the Caribbean. Try the Astro Orbiter in Tomorrowland, the Mad Tea Party in Fantasyland, or Goofy's Barnstormer in Mickey's Toontown Fair to observe how your child tolerates certain ride speeds and motions.

Do not assume that because an attraction is a theater presentation that it will not frighten your child. Trust us on this one: An attraction does not have to be moving to trigger unmitigated, panic-induced hysteria. Rides like the Big Thunder Mountain Railroad and Splash Mountain may look scary, but they do not have even one-fiftieth the potential for terrorizing children as do theater attractions like *Alien Encounter*. Before lining up for any attraction, be it a ride or a theater presentation, check out our description of it and see our Fright Factor list on pages 85–86.

2. Be Attuned to Peer and Parent Pressure   Sometimes young children will rise above their anxiety in an effort to please parents or siblings. This doesn't necessarily indicate a mastery of fear, much less enjoyment. If children leave a ride in apparently good shape, ask if they would like to go on it again (not necessarily now, but sometime). The response usually will indicate how much they actually enjoyed the experience. There's a big difference between having a good time and just mustering the courage to get through something.

3. Encourage and Empathize   Evaluating a child's capacity to handle the visual and tactile effects of Walt Disney World requires patience, understanding, and experimentation. Each of us, after all, has our own demons. If a child balks at or is frightened by a ride, respond constructively. Let your children know that lots of people, adults and children, are scared by what they see and feel. Help them understand that it's okay if they get frightened and that their fear doesn't lessen your love or respect. Take pains not to compound the discomfort by making a child feel inadequate; try not to undermine self-esteem, impugn courage, or ridicule. Most of all, don't induce guilt by suggesting the child's trepidation might be ruining the family's fun. It is also sometimes necessary to restrain older siblings' taunting or teasing.

A visit to Walt Disney World is more than just an outing or an adventure for a young child. It's a testing experience, a sort of controlled rite of passage. If you help your little one work through the challenges, the time can be immeasurably rewarding and a bonding experience for you both.

The Fright Factor

Of course, each youngster is different, but there are seven attraction elements that alone or combined could push a child's buttons:

1. Name of the Attraction   Young children will naturally be apprehensive about something called "The Haunted Mansion" or "The Tower of Terror."

2. Visual Impact of the Attraction from Outside   Splash Mountain and Big Thunder Mountain Railroad look scary enough to give even adults second thoughts, and they terrify many young children.

3. Visual Impact of the Indoor Queuing Area   Pirates of the Caribbean's caves and dungeons and The Haunted Mansion's "stretch rooms" can frighten children even before they board the ride.

4. Intensity of the Attraction   Some attractions are overwhelming, inundating the senses with sights, sounds, movement, and even smell. Epcot's *Honey, I Shrunk the Audience* and *It's Tough to Be a Bug* in the Animal Kingdom (no pun intended), for example, combine loud sounds, lasers, lights, and 3D cinematography to create a total sensory experience. For some preschoolers, this is two or three senses too many.

5. Visual Impact of the Attraction Itself   Sights in various attractions range from falling boulders to lurking buzzards, from grazing dinosaurs to attacking white blood cells. What one child calmly absorbs may scare the bejeebers out of another the same age.

6. Dark   Many Disney World attractions operate indoors in the dark. For some children, dark alone triggers fear. A child who is frightened on one dark ride (Snow White's Adventures, for example) may be unwilling to try other indoor rides.

7. The Ride Itself; the Tactile Experience   Some rides are wild enough to cause motion sickness, to wrench backs, and to discombobulate patrons of any age.

Disney Orientation Course

If your children are young enough to be frightened by the theme and content of Disney attractions (as opposed to the ride itself, which in certain cases can scare the owlpoop out of many adults), you need to get going on a Disney orientation course.

We receive many tips from parents telling how they prepared their young children for the Disney experience. A common strategy is to acquaint children with the characters and the stories behind the attractions by reading Disney books and watching Disney videos at home. A more direct approach is to rent Walt Disney World travel videos that show the actual attractions. Of the latter, a father from Arlington, Virginia, reports:

> *My kids both loved The Haunted Mansion, with appropriate preparation. We rented a tape before going so they could see it, and then I told them it was all "Mickey Mouse Magic" and that Mickey was just "joking you," to put it in their terms, and that there weren't any real ghosts, and that Mickey wouldn't let anyone actually get hurt.*

A mother from Teaneck, New Jersey, adds:

> *I rented movies to make my five-year-old more comfortable with rides* (Star Wars; Indiana Jones; Honey, I Shrunk the Kids). *We thought we might go to Universal, so I rented* King Kong, *and it is now my kid's favorite. If kids are afraid of rides in dark (like ours), buy a light-up toy and let them take it on the ride.*

A mother from Gloucester, Massachusetts, solved the fright problem on the spot:

> *The 3 ½-year-old liked It's a Small World, [but] was afraid of The Haunted Mansion. We just pulled his hat over his face and quietly talked to him while we enjoyed [the ride].*

PREPARING YOUR CHILDREN TO MEET THE CHARACTERS

Almost all Disney characters are quite large; several, like Brer Bear, are huge! Young children don't expect this, and preschoolers especially can be intimidated if not terrified.

Discuss the characters with your children before you go. If there is a high school or college with a costumed mascot nearby, arrange to let your kids check him out. If you don't have a mascot handy, then Santa Claus or the Easter Bunny will do.

On the first encounter at Walt Disney World, don't thrust your child at the character. Allow the little one to deal with this big

thing from whatever distance feels safe. If two adults are present, one should stay near the youngster while the other approaches the character and demonstrates that it's safe and friendly. Some kids warm to the characters immediately; some never do. Most take a little time and several encounters.

At Walt Disney World there are two kinds of characters: those whose costume includes a face-covering headpiece (animal characters and such humanlike characters as Captain Hook) and "face characters," those who resemble the characters, so no mask or headpiece is necessary. Face characters include Mary Poppins, Ariel, Jasmine, Aladdin, Cinderella, Belle, Snow White, Tarzan, Esmerelda, and Prince Charming.

Only face characters speak. Headpiece characters don't make noises of any kind. Because cast members couldn't possibly imitate the distinctive cinema voice of the character, Disney has determined that it's more effective to keep them silent. Lack of speech notwithstanding, headpiece characters are very warm and responsive, and communicate very effectively with gestures. Tell children in advance that headpiece characters don't talk.

Some character costumes are cumbersome and give cast members very poor visibility. (Eye holes frequently are in the mouth of the costume or even on the neck or chest.) This means characters are somewhat clumsy and have limited sight. Children who approach the character from the back or side may not be noticed, even if the child touches the character. It's possible in this situation for the character to accidentally step on the child or knock him or her down. It's best for a child to approach a character from the front, but occasionally not even this works. Duck characters (Donald, Daisy, Uncle Scrooge), for example, have to peer around their bills. If a character appears to be ignoring your child, pick up your child and hold him or her in front of the character until the character responds.

It's okay for your child to touch, pat, or hug the character. Understanding the unpredictability of children, the character will keep his feet very still, particularly refraining from moving backward or sideways. Most characters will sign autographs or pose for pictures. If your child wants to collect character autographs, it's a good idea to carry a pen the width of a magic marker. Costumes make it exceedingly difficult for characters to wield a pen, so the bigger the writing instrument, the better.

ROLE PLAYING

Especially for younger children, role playing is a great way to inculcate vital lessons concerning safety, contingency situations, and potential danger. Play "what would you do if" for a variety of scenarios including getting lost, being approached by strangers, getting help if mommy is sick, and so on. Children have incredible recall when its comes to role playing with siblings and parents, and are much more likely to respond appropriately in an actual situation than they will if the same information is presented in a lecture.

Physical Preparation

You'll find that some physical conditioning coupled with a realistic sense of the toll that Walt Disney World takes on your body will preclude falling apart in the middle of your vacation. As one of our readers put it, "If you pay attention to eat, heat, feet, and sleep, you'll be OK."

As you contemplate the stamina of your family, it's important to understand that somebody is going to run out of steam first, and when they do the whole family will be affected. Sometimes a cold drink or a snack will revive the flagging member. Sometimes, however, no amount of cajoling or treats will work. In this situation it's crucial that you recognize that the child, grandparent, or spouse is at the end of his or her rope. The correct decision is to get them back to the hotel. Pushing the exhausted beyond their capacity will spoil the day for them—and you. Accept that stamina and energy levels vary and be prepared to administer to members of your family who poop out. One more thing: no guilt trips. "We've driven a thousand miles to take you to Disney World and now you're going to ruin everything!" is not an appropriate response.

THE AGONY OF THE FEET

Here's a little factoid to chew on: If you spend a day at Epcot and visit both sections of the park, you will walk five to nine miles! The walking, however, will be nothing like a five-mile hike in the woods. At Epcot (and the other Disney parks as well) you will be in direct sunlight most of the time, will have to navigate through huge jostling crowds, will be walking on hot pavement, and will have to endure waits in line between bursts of walking. The bottom line, if you haven't figured it out, is that Disney theme parks (especially in the summer) are not for wimps!

Though most children are active, their normal play usually doesn't condition them for the exertion of touring a Disney theme park. We recommend starting a program of family walks six weeks or more before your trip. A Pennsylvania mom who did just that offers the following:

> We had our six-year-old begin walking with us a bit every day one month before leaving—when we arrived [at Walt Disney World] her little legs could carry her and she had a lot of stamina.

The first thing you need to do, immediately after making your hotel reservation, is to get thee to a footery. Take the whole family to a shoe store and buy each member the best pair of walking, hiking, or running shoes you can afford. Wear exactly the kind of socks to try on the shoes as you will wear when using them to hike. Do not under any circumstances attempt to tour Walt Disney World shod in sandals, flip-flops, loafers, or any kind of high heel or platform shoe.

Good socks are as important as good shoes. When you walk, your feet sweat like a mule in a peat bog, and moisture increases friction. To minimize friction, wear two pairs of socks. The pair next to your feet should ideally be polypropylene thin socks or sock liners. The outer sock can be either a natural fiber like cotton or wool, or a synthetic fiber. To further combat moisture, dust your feet with some anti-fungal talcum powder. If your children (or you, for that matter) do not consider it cool to wear socks, get over it! Bare feet, whether encased in Nikes, Weejuns, Docksiders, or Birkenstocks, will turn into lumps of throbbing red meat if you tackle a Disney park without socks.

All right, now you've got some good shoes and socks. The next thing is to break the shoes in. This can be accomplished painlessly by wearing the shoes in the course of normal activities for about three weeks.

Once the shoes are broken in it's time to start walking. The whole family will need to toughen up their feet and build endurance. As you begin, remember that little people have little strides, and though your six-year-old may create the appearance of running circles around you, consider that (1) he won't have the stamina to go at that pace very long, and (2) more to the point, he probably has to take two strides or so to every one of yours to keep up when you walk together.

Start by taking short walks around the neighborhood, walking on pavement, and increasing the distance about a quarter of a mile on each outing. Older children will shape up quickly. Younger children should build endurance more slowly and incrementally. Increase distance until you can manage a six- or seven-mile hike without requiring CPR. And remember, you're not training to be able walk six or seven miles just once: At Walt Disney World you will be hiking five to seven miles and more almost *every day*. So unless you plan to crash after the first day, you've got to prepare your feet to walk long distances for three to five consecutive days.

Let's be honest and admit up front that not all feet are created equal. Some folks are blessed with really tough feet, whereas the feet of others sprout blisters if you look at them sideways. Assuming that there's nothing wrong with either shoes or socks, a few brisk walks will clue you in to what kind of feet your family have. If you have a tenderfoot in your family, walks of incrementally increased distances will usually toughen up his or her feet to some extent. Be sure to give him or her adequate recovery time between walks (48 hours will usually be enough), however, or you'll make the problem worse. For those whose feet refuse to toughen, your only alternative is preventive care. After several walks, you will know where your tenderfoot tends to develop blisters. If you can anticipate where the blisters will develop, you can cover the sensitive spots in advance with moleskin, a friction-resistant adhesive dressing. Spenco second skin does essentially the same thing.

When you initiate your walking program, teach your children to tell you if they feel a "hot spot" on their feet. This is the warning that a blister is developing. If your kids are too young, too oblivious, too preoccupied, or don't understand the concept, your best bet is to make regular feet checks. Have your children remove their shoes and socks and present their feet for inspection. Look for red spots and blisters, and ask if they have any places on their feet that hurt. If your child is age eight or younger, we recommend regular feet inspections whether he or she understands the hot spot idea or not. Even the brightest and most well-intended child will fail to sound off when distracted.

During your conditioning and also at Walt Disney World carry a foot emergency kit in your daypack or hip pack. The kit should contain gauze, Betadyne antibiotic ointment, moleskin or Spenco second skin, scissors, a sewing needle or some such to drain blisters as well as matches to sterilize the needle. An extra pair of dry socks and talc are optional.

If you discover a hot spot, dry the foot and cover the spot immediately with moleskin or Spenco second skin. Cut the covering large enough to cover the skin surrounding the hot spot. If you find that a blister has already developed, first air out and dry the foot. Next, using your sterile needle, drain the fluid but do not remove the top skin. Clean the area with your Betadyne, place a gauze square over the blister, and cover the whole enchilada with moleskin. If you do not have moleskin or Spenco second skin, do not try to cover the hot spot or blister with Band-Aids. Band-Aids slip and wad up.

If you have a child who will physically fit in a stroller, rent one, no matter how well conditioned your family is. The stroller will provide the child the option of walking or riding, and, if he collapses, you won't have to carry him. Even if your child hardly uses the stroller at all, it serves as a convenient rolling depository for water bottles and other stuff you may not feel like carrying. Strollers at Walt Disney World are covered in detail on pages 139–142.

SLEEP, REST, AND RELAXATION

OK, we know that this section is about physical preparation *before you go*, but this concept is so absolutely critical that we need to tattoo it on your brain right now.

Physical conditioning is important, but is *not* a substitute for adequate rest. Even marathon runners need recovery time. If you push too hard and try to do too much, you'll either crash or, at a minimum, turn what should be fun into an ordeal. Rest means plenty of sleep at night, naps during the afternoon on most days, and planned breaks in your vacation itinerary. And don't forget that the brain needs rest and relaxation as well as the body. The stimulation inherent in touring a Disney theme park is enough to put most children and many adults into system overload. It is imperative that you remove your family from this unremitting assault on the senses, preferably for part of each day, and do something relaxing and quiet like swimming or reading.

The theme parks are huge; don't try to see everything in one day. Tour in early morning and return to your hotel around 11:30 a.m. for lunch, a swim, and a nap. Even during off-season when the crowds are smaller and the temperature more pleasant, the size of the major theme parks will exhaust most children under age eight by lunchtime. Return to the park in late afternoon or early evening and continue touring. A family from Texas underlines the importance of naps and rest:

> *Despite not following any of your "tours," we did follow the theme of visiting a specific park in the morning, leaving midafternoon for either a nap back at the room or a trip to the Dixie Landings pool, and then returning to one of the parks in the evening. On the few occasions when we skipped your advice, I was muttering to myself by dinner. I can't tell you what I was muttering. . . .*

When it comes to naps, this mom does not mince words:

> *One last thing for parents of small kids—take the book's advice and get out of the park and take the nap, take the nap, TAKE THE NAP! Never in my life have I seen so many parents screaming at, ridiculing, or slapping their kids. (What a vacation!) WDW is overwhelming for kids and adults. Even though the rental strollers recline for sleeping, we noticed that most of the toddlers and preschoolers didn't give up and sleep until 5 p.m., several hours after the fun had worn off, and right about the time their parents wanted them to be awake and polite in a restaurant.*

A mom from Rochester, New York, was equally adamant:

> *[You] absolutely must rest during the day. Kids went from 8 a.m. to 9 p.m. in the Magic Kingdom. Kids did great that day, but we were all completely worthless the next day. Definitely must pace yourself. Don't ever try to do two full days of park sightseeing in a row. Rest during the day. Go to a water park or sleep in every other day.*

If you plan to return to your hotel in midday and would like your room made up, let housekeeping know.

Bibbity-Bobbity Buzz-cut

Before you leave home get each of your children a short haircut. Not only will they be cooler and more comfortable, but especially with your girls, you'll save them (and you) the hassle of tangles and about 20 minutes of foo-fooing a day.

Organizational Preparation

Allow your children to participate in the planning of your time at Walt Disney World. Guide them diplomatically through the options, establishing advance decisions about what to do each day and how the day will be structured. Begin with your trip *to* Walt Disney World, deciding what time to depart, who sits by the window, whether to stop for meals or eat in the car, and so on. For the Walt Disney World part of your vacation, build consensus for wake-up call, bedtime, building naps into the itinerary, and establish ground rules for eating, buying snacks and refreshments, and shopping. Determine the order for visiting the different theme parks and make a list of "must-see" attractions.

Generally it's better to just sketch in the broad strokes on the master plan. The detail of what to do when you actually arrive at the park can be decided the night before you go, or with the help of one of our touring plans once you get there. Above all, be flexible. Don't get obsessed with any of the plans, especially the touring part. It's your vacation, after all, and you can amend (or even scrap) the plan if you want. One important caveat, however: Make sure you keep any promises or agreements that you make when planning. They may not seem important to you, but they will to your children, who will remember for a long, long time that you let them down.

To keep your thinking fresh and to adequately cover all bases, develop your plan in a series of family meetings that do not exceed 30 minutes each. You'll discover that all members of the family will devote a lot of thought to the plan both in and between meetings. Don't try to anticipate every conceivable contingency or you'll end up with something as detailed and unworkable as the tax code.

The more you can agree to and nail down in advance, the less potential you'll have for disagreement and confrontation once you arrive. Because children are more comfortable with the tangible than the conceptual, and also because they sometimes have short memories, we recommend typing up all of your decisions and agreements and providing a copy to each child. Create a fun document, not a legalistic one. You'll find that your children will review it in anticipation of all the things they will see and do, will consult it often, and will even read it to the younger children.

By now you're probably wondering what one of these documents looks like, so here's a sample. Incidentally, this itinerary reflects the preferences of its creators, the Shelton family, and is not meant to be offered as an example of an ideal itinerary. It does, however, incorporate many of our most basic and strongly held recommendations, such as setting limits and guidelines in advance, getting enough rest, getting to the theme parks early, touring the theme parks in shorter visits with naps and swimming in between, and saving time and money by having a cooler full of food for breakfast. As you will see, the Sheltons go pretty much full-tilt without much unstructured time and will probably be exhausted by the time they get home, but that's their choice. One more thing—the Sheltons visited Walt Disney World in late June when all of the theme parks stay open late.

THE GREAT 1999 WALT DISNEY WORLD EXPEDITION

Co-Captains   Mary and Jack Shelton

Team Members   Lynn and Jimmy Shelton

Expedition Funding   The main Expedition Fund will cover everything except personal purchases. Each team member will receive $35 for souvenirs and personal purchases. Anything above $35 will be paid for by team members with their own money.

Expedition Gear   Each team member will wear an official expedition T-shirt and carry a hip pack.

Pre-Departure   Jack makes priority seating* arrangements at Walt Disney World restaurants. Mary, Lynn, and Jimmy make up trail mix and other snacks for the hip packs.

Itinerary:

Day 1: Friday

6:30 p.m.	Dinner
After dinner	Pack car
10 p.m.	Lights out

Day 2: Saturday

7 a.m.	Wake up!
7:15 a.m.	Breakfast
8 a.m.	Depart Chicago for Hampton Inn North, 11 Elm St., Chattanooga, TN; (615) 235-9843; Confirmation # DE56432; Lynn rides shotgun
About noon	Stop for lunch; Jimmy picks restaurant
7 p.m.	Dinner
9:30 p.m.	Lights out

Day 3: Sunday

7 a.m.	Wake up!
7:30 a.m.	Breakfast
8:15 a.m.	Depart Chattanooga for Walt Disney World, Dixie Landings Resort; (407) 934-6000; Confirmation # L124532; Jimmy rides shotgun
About noon	Stop for lunch; Lynn picks restaurant
5 p.m.	Check in, buy park admissions, and unpack
6–7 p.m.	Mary and Jimmy shop for breakfast food for cooler
7:15 p.m.	Dinner at Boatwright's at Dixie Landings
After dinner	Walk along Bonnet Creek
10 p.m.	Lights out

Day 4: Monday

7 a.m.	Wake up! Cold breakfast from cooler in room
8 a.m.	Depart room to catch bus for Epcot
Noon	Lunch at Epcot
1 p.m.	Return to hotel for swimming and a nap
5 p.m.	Return to Epcot for touring, dinner, and *IllumiNations*
9:30 p.m.	Return to hotel
10:30 p.m.	Lights out

Day 5: Tuesday

7 a.m.	Wake up! Cold breakfast from cooler in room
7:45 a.m.	Depart room to catch bus for Disney-MGM Studios
Noon	Lunch at Studios
2:30 p.m.	Return to hotel for swimming and a nap
6 p.m.	Drive car to dinner at Whispering Canyon Cafe at the Wilderness Lodge
7:30 p.m.	Return to Studios via car for touring and *Fantasmic!*
10 p.m.	Return to hotel
11 p.m.	Lights out

Day 6: Wednesday

ZZZZZZ!	Lazy morning—sleep in!
10:30 a.m.	Late-morning swim
Noon	Lunch at Dixie Landings food court
1 p.m.	Depart room to catch bus for Animal Kingdom Tour until Animal Kingdom closes
8 p.m.	Dinner at Rainforest Cafe at Animal Kingdom
9:15 p.m.	Return to hotel via bus
10:30 p.m.	Lights out

Day 7: Thursday

6 a.m.	Wake up! Cold breakfast from cooler in room
6:45 a.m.	Depart room to catch bus for early entry at Magic Kingdom
11:30 a.m.	Return to hotel for lunch, swimming, and a nap
4:45 p.m.	Drive to Contemporary Resort for dinner at Chef Mickey's
6:15 p.m.	Walk from the Contemporary to the Magic Kingdom for more touring, fireworks, and parade
11 p.m.	Return to Contemporary via walkway or monorail; get car and return to hotel
11:45 p.m.	Lights out

Day 8: Friday

8 a.m.	Wake up! Cold breakfast from cooler in room
8:40 a.m.	Drive to Blizzard Beach water park
Noon	Lunch at Blizzard Beach
1:30 p.m.	Return to hotel for nap and packing
4 p.m.	Revisit favorite park or do whatever we want
Dinner	When and where we decide
10 p.m.	Return to hotel
10:30 p.m.	Lights out

Day 9: Saturday

7:30 a.m.	Wake up!
8:30 a.m.	Depart for home after fast-food breakfast with overnight in Nashville, Executive Inn, 124 Wiley Parkway; (615) 453-6207; Confirmation # SD234; Lynn rides shotgun
About noon	Stop for lunch; Jimmy picks restaurant
7 p.m.	Dinner
10 p.m.	Lights out

Day 10: Sunday

7 a.m.	Wake up!
7:45 a.m.	Depart for home after fast-food breakfast; Jimmy rides shotgun
About noon	Stop for lunch; Lynn picks restaurant for lunch
4:30 p.m.	Home Sweet Home!

Notice that the Sheltons' itinerary provides minimal structure and maximum flexibility. It specifies which park the family will tour each day without attempting to nail down exactly what the family will do there. No matter how detailed your itinerary is, be prepared for surprises at Walt Disney World, both good and bad.

---

* A priority seating is not a reservation, although you must specify an arrival time. It means simply that you will be seated ahead of walk-in customers. For some of the more popular Disney restaurants, however, it's almost impossible to get a table without a priority seating. If you decide in advance where (and when) you want to eat, you can make your priority seatings before you leave home by calling (407) WDW DINE.

If an unforeseen event renders part of the plan useless or imprac-tical, just roll with it. And always remember that it's *your* itiner-ary: You created it and you can change it. Just try to make any changes the result of family discussion and be especially careful not to scrap an element of the plan that your children perceive as something you promised them.

Routines That Travel   If you observe certain routines at home—for example, reading a book before bed or having a bath first thing in the morning—try to incorporate these familiar activities into your vacation schedule. They will provide your children with a sense of security and normalcy.

Logistic Preparation

When I recently launched into my spiel about good logistic prepa-ration for a Walt Disney World vacation, a friend from Indi-anapolis said, "Wait, what's the big deal? You pack clothes, a few games for the car, then go!" So OK, I confess, that will work, but life can be sweeter and the vacation smoother (as well as less expen-sive) with the right gear.

CLOTHING

Let's start with clothes. We recommend springing for vacation uniforms. Buy for each child several sets of jeans (or shorts) and T-shirts, all matching, and all the same. For a one-week trip, as an example, get each child three or so pair of khaki shorts, three or so light yellow T-shirts, and a pair of clean white socks for each day. What's the point? First, you don't have to play fashion designer, coordinating a week's worth of stylish combos. Each morning the kids put on their uniform. It's simple, it's time sav-ing, there are no decisions to make and no arguments about what to wear. Second, uniforms make your children easier to spot and keep together in the theme parks. Third, the uniforms give your family, as well as the vacation itself, some added identity. If you're like the Shelton family who created the sample itinerary in the section on organizational planning, you might go so far as to cre-ate a logo for the trip to be printed on the shirts.

When it comes to buying your uniforms, we have a few sug-gestions. Purchase well-made, durable shorts or jeans that will serve your children well beyond the vacation. Active children can never have too many pairs of shorts or jeans. As far as the T-shirts go, buy short-sleeve shirts in light colors for warm weather, or long-sleeve, darker-colored T-shirts for cooler weather. We suggest that you purchase your colored shirts from a local T-shirt printing company. Cleverly listed under "T-shirts" (sometimes under "Screen Printing") in the Yellow Pages, these firms will be happy to sell you either printed T-shirts or unprinted T-shirts (called "blanks") with long or short sleeves. You can select from a wide choice of colors not generally available in retail clothing stores, and will not have to worry about finding the sizes you need. Plus, the shirts will cost a fraction of what a clothing retailer will charge. Most shirts come in the more durable 100% cotton or in the more wrinkle-resistant 50% cotton and 50% polyester (50/50s). The cotton shirts are a little cooler and more comfortable in hot, humid weather. The 50/50s dry a bit faster if they get wet.

Labels   A great idea, especially for younger children, is to attach labels with your family name, home town, the name of your hotel, and the dates of your stay inside the shirt, for example:

Carlton Family of Frankfort, KY
Port Orleans; 5–12 May, 2000

Instruct your smaller children to show the label to an adult if they get separated from you. Elimination of the child's first name (which most children of talking age can articulate in any event) allows you to order labels that are all the same, that can be used by anyone in the family, and that can also be affixed to such easily lost items as caps, hats, jackets, hip packs, ponchos, and umbrellas. Folks who make custom labels are listed in the Yellow Pages under "Embroidery." The screen printer who sells you Tshirts may also be able to provide labels. If fooling with labels sounds like too much of a hassle, check out "When Kids Get Lost" (pages 142–144) for some alternatives.

Dressing for Cooler Weather   Central Florida experiences temperatures all over the scale from November through March, so it could be a bit chilly if you visit during those months. Our suggestion is to layer, for example a breathable, waterproof or water-resistant windbreaker over a light, long-sleeved polypro shirt, over a long-sleeved T-shirt. As with the baffles of a sleeping bag or down coat, it is the air trapped between the layers that keeps you warm. If all the layers are thin, you won't be left with something bulky to cart around if you want to pull one or more off. Later in this section, we'll advocate wearing a hip pack. Each layer should be sufficiently compactible to fit easily in that hip pack along with whatever else is in it.

ACCESSORIES

I wanted to call this part "Belts and Stuff," but the editor (who obviously spends a lot of time at Macy's) thought "Accessories" put a finer point on it. In any event, we recommend pants for your children with reinforced elastic waistbands that eliminate the need to wear a belt (one less thing to try to find when you're trying to leave). If your children like belts or want to carry an item that is suspended from a belt, buy them military-style 1½-wide web belts at any army/navy surplus or camping equipment store. The belts weigh less than half as much as leather, are cooler, and are washable.

Sunglasses   The Florida sun is so bright and the glare so blinding that we recommend sunglasses for every member of the family. For children and adults of all ages, a good accessory item is a polypro eyeglass strap for spectacles or sunglasses. The best models have a little device that allows you to adjust the amount of slack in the strap. This allows your child to comfortably hang sunglasses from his or her neck when indoors or, alternately, to secure them fast to his or her head while experiencing a fast ride outdoors.

Hip Packs and Wallets   Unless you are touring with an infant or toddler, the largest thing anyone in your family should carry is a hip pack, or fanny pack. Each adult and child should have one. They should be large enough to carry at least a half-day's worth of snacks as well as other items deemed necessary (Chap Stick, bandanna, antibacterial hand gel, and so on) and still have enough room left to stash a hat, poncho, or light windbreaker. We recommend buying full-sized hip packs at outdoor retailers as opposed to small, child-sized hip packs. The packs are light, can be made to fit any child large enough to tote a hip pack; have slip-resistant, comfortable, wide belting; and will last for years.

Do not carry billfolds or wallets, car keys, Disney Resort IDs, or room keys in your hip packs. We usually give this advice because hip packs are vulnerable to thieves (who snip them off and run), but pickpocketing and theft are not all that common at Walt Disney World. In this instance, the advice stems from a tendency of children to inadvertently drop their wallet in the process of rummaging around in their hip packs for snacks and other items.

Incidentally, unless you advise the front desk to the contrary, all Disney resort room keys can be used for park admission and as credit cards. They are definitely something you don't want to lose. Our advice is to void the charge privileges on your preteen children's cards and then collect them and put them together someplace safe when not in use.

You should weed through your billfold and remove to a safe place anything that you will not need on your vacation (family photos, local library card, department store credit cards, business cards, movie rental ID cards, and so on). In addition to having a lighter wallet to lug around, you will decrease your

exposure in the event that your wallet is lost or stolen. When we are working at Walt Disney World, we carry a small profile billfold with a driver's license, a Visa card, our Disney Resort room key, and a small amount of cash. Think about it: You don't need anything else.

Day Packs We see a lot of folks at Walt Disney World carrying day packs (that is, small, frameless backpacks) and/or water bottle belts that strap around your waist. Day packs might be a good choice if you plan to carry a lot of camera equipment or if you need to carry baby supplies on your person. Otherwise, try to travel as light as possible. Packs are hot, cumbersome, not very secure, and must be removed every time you get on a ride or sit down for a show. Hip packs, by way of contrast, can simply be rotated around the waist from your back to your abdomen if you need to sit down. Additionally, our observation has been that the contents of one day pack can usually be redistributed to two or so hip packs (except in the case of camera equipment).

Caps We do not recommend caps (or hats of any kind) for children unless they are especially sun sensitive. Simply put, kids pull caps on and off as they enter and exit attractions, rest rooms, and restaurants, and . . . big surprise, they lose them. In fact, they lose them by the thousands. You could provide a ball cap for every Little Leaguer in America from the caps that are lost at Walt Disney World each summer.

If your children are partial to caps, there is a device sold at ski and camping supply stores that might increase the likelihood of the cap returning home with the child. Essentially, it's a short, light cord with little alligator clips on both ends. Hook one clip to the shirt collar and the other to the hat. It's a great little invention: I use one when I ski in case my ball cap blows off.

Rain Gear Rain in central Florida is a fact of life, although persistent rain day after day is unusual (it is the Sunshine State, after all!). Our suggestion is to check out the Weather Channel or weather forecasts on the Internet for three or so days before you leave home to see if there are any major storm systems heading for central Florida. Weather forecasting has improved to the extent that predictions concerning systems and fronts four to seven days out are now pretty reliable. If it appears that you might see some rough weather during your visit, you're better off bringing rain gear from home. If nothing big weatherwise is on the horizon, however, you can take your chances.

We at the *Unofficial Guide* usually do not bring rain gear. First, scattered thundershowers are more the norm than are prolonged periods of rain. Second, rain gear, especially ponchos, are pretty cheap (about $5) at Walt Disney World and are available in seemingly every retail shop. Third, in the theme parks, a surprising number of attractions and queuing areas are under cover. Fourth, we prefer to travel light.

If you do find yourself in a big storm, however, you'll want to have both a poncho and an umbrella. As one *Unofficial* reader put it, "Umbrellas make the rain much more bearable. When rain isn't beating down on your ponchoed head, it's easier to ignore."

An advantage of buying ponchos before you leave home is that you can choose the color. At Walt Disney World all the ponchos are bright yellow, and it's quite a sight when 30,000 differently clad individuals suddenly transform themselves into what looks like an army of sumo killer bees. If your family is wearing blue ponchos, they'll be easier to spot.

Finally, equip each child with a big bandanna. Although bandannas come in handy for wiping noses, scouring ice cream from chins and mouths, and dabbing sweat from the forehead, they can also be tied around the neck to protect from sunburn.

And consider this tip from a Memphis, Tennessee, mom:

Scotchgard your shoes. The difference is unbelievable.

MISCELLANEOUS ITEMS

Medication   Some parents of hyperactive children on medication discontinue or decrease the child's normal dosage at the end of the school year. If you have such a child, be aware that Walt Disney World might overly stimulate him or her. Consult your physician before altering your child's medication regimen.

Sunscreen   Overheating and sunburn are among the most common problems of younger children at Walt Disney World. Carry and use sunscreen SPF 15 or higher. Be sure to put some on children in strollers, even if the stroller has a canopy. Some of the worst cases of sunburn we've seen were on the exposed foreheads and feet of toddlers and infants in strollers. Protect skin from overexposure. To avoid overheating, rest regularly in the shade or in an air-conditioned restaurant or show.

Water Bottles   Don't count on keeping young children hydrated with soft drinks and stops at water fountains. Long lines may hamper buying refreshments, and fountains may not be handy. Furthermore, excited children may not realize or tell you that they're thirsty or hot. We recommend renting a stroller for children age six and younger and carrying plastic bottles of water. Plastic squeeze bottles with caps are sold in all major parks for about $3.

Coolers and Mini-Fridges   If you drive to Walt Disney World, bring two coolers: a small one for drinks in the car, and a large one for the hotel room. If you fly and rent a car, stop and purchase a large Styrofoam cooler, which can be discarded at the end of the trip. If you will be without a car, rent a mini-fridge from your hotel. At Disney resorts, mini-refrigerators cost about $5 a day. Make sure you reserve one when you book your room.

Coolers and mini-fridges allow you to have breakfast in your hotel room, store snacks and lunch supplies to take to the theme parks, and supplant expensive vending machines for snacks and beverages at the hotel. To keep the contents of your cooler cold, we suggest freezing a two-gallon milk jug full of water before you head out. In a good cooler, it will take the jug five or more days to thaw. If you buy a Styrofoam cooler in Florida, you can use bagged ice supplemented by ice from the ice machine at your hotel. Even if you have to rent a mini-fridge, you will save a bundle of cash as well as significant time by reducing dependence on restaurant meals and expensive snacks and drinks purchased from vendors.

Food Prep Kit   If you plan to make sandwiches, bring along your favorite condiments and seasonings from home. A typical travel kit will include mayonnaise, catsup, mustard, salt and pepper, and packets of sugar or artificial sweetener. Also throw in some plastic knives and spoons, paper napkins, plastic cups, and a box of Baggies. For breakfast you will need some plastic bowls for cereal. Of course, you can buy this stuff in Florida, but you probably won't consume it all, so why waste the money? If you drink bottled beer or wine, bring a bottle opener and corkscrew.

Electronics   Regardless of your children's ages, always bring a nightlight. Flashlights are also handy for finding stuff in a dark hotel room after the kids are asleep. If you are big coffee drinkers and if you drive, bring along a coffeemaker.

Walkmans and portable CD players with headphones as well as some electronic games are often controversial gear for a family outing. We recommend compromise. Headphones can allow kids to create their own space even when they're with others, and that can be a safety valve. That said, try to agree before the trip on some headphone parameters so you don't begin to feel as if they're being used to keep other family members and the trip itself at a distance. If you're traveling by car, take turns choosing the radio station, CD, or audiotape for part of the trip.

An increasing number of readers stay in touch while on vacation by using walkie talkies. Here's what they have to say:

From a Cabot, Arkansas, family:

> *Borrow or get walkie talkies! The vacation is expensive enough so get some walkie talkies! Our youngest was too scared or too short for some rides, plus I was expecting, so we would sit outside or go to a snack area but were always in contact. My husband, Joe, could tell me how long the wait was, when he was about to come down Splash Mountain (for me to take a photo!), or where to meet.*

Concerning the walkie-talkie's, a dad from Roanoke, Virginia, is on the same wavelength:

> *The single best purchase we made was to get the Motorola TalkAbout walkie-talkies. They have a two mile range and are about the size of a deck of cards. We first started using them at the airport when I was checking the bags and she took the kids off to the gate. At the parks, the kids would invariably have diverse interests. With the walkie-talkies, however, we easily could split up and simply communicate with each other when we wanted to meet back up. At least half-dozen times, exasperated parents asked where they could rent/buy the walkie-talkies.*

Don't Forget the Tent   This is not a joke and has nothing to do with camping. When my daughter was preschool age we about went crazy trying to get her to sleep in our shared hotel room. She was accustomed to having her own room at home and was hyperstimulated whenever we traveled. We tried makeshift curtains and room dividers and even rearranged the furniture in a few hotel rooms to create the illusion of a more private, separate space for her. It was all for naught. It wasn't until she was around four years old and we took her camping that we seized on an idea that had some promise. She liked the cozy, secure, womb-like feel of a backpacking tent, and quieted down much more readily than she ever had in hotel rooms. So, the next time we stayed in a hotel, we pitched our backpacking tent in the corner of the room. In she went, nested for a bit, and fell asleep.

Since the time of my daughter's childhood, there has been an astounding evolution in tent design. Responding to the needs of climbers and paddlers who often have to pitch tents on rocks (where it's impossible to drive stakes), tent manufactures developed a broad range of tents with self-supporting frames that can be erected virtually anywhere without ropes or stakes. Affordable and sturdy, many are as simple to put up as opening an umbrella. So, if your child is too young for a room of his or her own, or you can't afford a second hotel room, try pitching a small tent. Modern tents are self-contained with floors and an entrance that can be zipped up (or not) for privacy, but cannot be locked. Kids appreciate having their own space and enjoy the adventure of being in a tent, even one set up in the corner of a hotel room. Sizes range from children's "play tents" with a 2 ½' × 3' base to models large enough to sleep two or three husky teens. Light and compactible when stored, a two-adult-size tent in its own storage bag (called a "stuffsack") will take up about one-fifth or less of a standard overhead bin on a commercial airliner. Another option for infants and toddlers is to drape a sheet over your portable crib or playpen to make a tent.

The Box On one memorable Walt Disney World excursion when my children were younger, we started each morning with an immensely annoying, involuntary scavenger hunt. Invariably, seconds before our scheduled departure to the theme park, we discovered that some combination of shoes, billfolds, sunglasses, hip packs, or other necessities were unaccountably missing. For the next 15 minutes we would root through the room like pigs hunting truffles in an attempt to locate the absent items. Now I don't know about your kids, but when my kids lost a shoe or something, they always searched where it was easiest to look, as opposed to where the lost article was most likely to be. I would be jammed under a bed feeling around while my children stood in the middle of the room intently inspecting the ceiling. As my friends will tell you, I'm as open to a novel theory as the next guy, but we never did find any shoes on the ceiling. Not once. Anyway, here's what I finally did: I swung by a liquor store and mooched a big empty box. From then on, every time we returned to the room, I had the kids deposit shoes, hip packs, and other potentially wayward items in the box. After that the box was off limits until the next morning when I doled out the contents.

Plastic Garbage Bags   There are two attractions, the Kali River Rapids raft ride in the Animal Kingdom, and Splash Mountain in the Magic Kingdom, where you are certain to get wet and possibly soaked. If it's really hot and you don't care, then fine. But if it's cool or you're just not up for a soaking, bring a large plastic trash bag to the park. By cutting holes in the top and on the sides you can fashion a sack poncho that will keep your clothes from getting wet. On the raft ride, you will also get your feet wet. If your not up for walking around in squishing, soaked shoes, bring a second, smaller plastic bag to wear over your feet while riding.

SUPPLIES FOR INFANTS AND TODDLERS

Based on recommendations from hundreds of *Unofficial Guide* readers, here's what we suggest you carry with you when touring with infants and toddlers:

- A disposable diaper for every hour you plan to be away from your hotel room

- A plastic (vinyl) diaper wrap with Velcro closures

- A cloth diaper or kitchen towel to put over your shoulder for burping

- Two receiving blankets: one to wrap the baby, one to lay baby on or to drape over you when you nurse

- Ointment for diaper rash

- Moistened towelettes such as Handi Wipes

- Prepared formula in bottles if you are not breast feeding

- A washable bib, baby spoon, and baby food if your infant is eating solids

- For toddlers, a small toy for comfort and to keep them occupied during attractions

Baby Care Centers at the theme parks will sell you just about anything that you forget or run out of. Like all things Disney, prices will be higher than elsewhere, but at least you won't need to detour to a drug store in the middle of your touring day.

Remembering Your Trip

1. Purchase a notebook for each child and spend some time each evening recording the events of the day. If your children have trouble getting motivated or don't know what to write about, start a discussion; otherwise, let them write or draw whatever they want to remember from the day's events.

2. Collect mementos along the way and create a treasure box in a small tin or cigar box. Months or years later, it's fun to look at postcards, seashells, or ticket stubs to jump-start a memory.

3. Add inexpensive postcards to your photographs to create an album, then write a few words on each page to accompany the images.

4. Give each child a disposable camera to record his or her version of the trip. One five-year-old snapped an entire series of photos that never showed anyone above the waist—his view of the world (and the photos are priceless).

5. Nowadays, many families travel with a camcorder, though we recommend using one sparingly—parents end up viewing the trip through the lens rather than enjoying the sights. If you must, take it along, but only record a few moments of major sights (too much is boring anyway). And let the kids tape and narrate.

6. Another inexpensive way to record memories is a palm-size tape recorder. Let all family members describe their experiences. Hearing a small child's voice years later is so endearing, and those recorded descriptions will trigger an album's worth of memories, far more focused than what many novices capture with a camcorder.

Finally, when it comes to taking photos and collecting mementos, don't let the tail wag the dog. You are not going to Walt Disney World to build the biggest scrapbook in history. Or as this Houston mom put it,

Tell your readers to get a grip on the photography thing. We were so busy shooting pictures that we kind of lost the thread. We had to get our pictures developed when we got home to see what all we did [while on vacation].

Trial Run

If you give thoughtful consideration to all areas of mental, physical, organizational, and logistical preparation discussed in this chapter, what remains is to familiarize yourself with Walt Disney World itself, and of course, to conduct your field test. Yep, that's right, we want you to take the whole platoon on the road for a day to see if you are combat ready. No joke, this is important: You'll learn who poops out first, who is prone to developing blisters, who has to pee every 11 seconds, and given the proper forum, how compatible your family is in terms of what you like to see and do.

For the most informative trial run, choose a local venue that requires lots of walking, dealing with crowds, and making decisions on how to spend your time. Regional theme parks and state fairs are your best bets, followed by large zoos and museums. Devote the whole day. Kick off the morning with an early start, just like you will at Walt Disney World, paying attention to who's organized and ready to go and who's dragging his or her butt and holding up the group. If you have to drive an hour or two to get to your test venue, no big deal: you'll have to do some commuting at Walt Disney World, too. Spend the whole day, eat a couple meals, stay late.

Don't bias the sample (that is, mess with the outcome) by telling everyone you are practicing for Walt Disney World. Everyone behaves differently when they know they are being tested or evaluated. Your objective is not to run a perfect drill, but to find out as much as you can about how the individuals in your family, as well as the family as a group, respond to and deal with everything they experience during the day. Pay attention to who moves quickly and who is slow; to who is adventuresome and who is reticent; to who keeps going and who needs frequent rest breaks; to who sets the agenda and who is content to follow; to who is easily agitated and who stays cool; to who tends to dawdle or wander off; to who is curious and who is bored; to who is demanding and who is accepting. You get the idea.

Discuss the findings of the test run with your spouse the next day. Don't be discouraged if your test day wasn't perfect; few (if any) are. Distinguish between problems that are remedial and problems that are intrinsic to your family's emotional or physical makeup (no amount of hiking, for example, will toughen up some people's feet).

Establish a plan for addressing remedial problems (further conditioning, setting limits before you go, trying harder to achieve family consensus, whatever) and develop strategies for minimizing or working around problems that are a fact of life (waking sleepyheads 15 minutes early, placing moleskin on likely blister sites before setting out, packing familiar food for the toddler who balks at restaurant fare). If you are an attentive observer, a fair diagnostician, and a creative problem solver, you'll be able to work out a significant percentage of the problems you're likely to encounter at Walt Disney World before you ever leave home.

Part Five

Get in the Boat, Men!

This is not a *Jeopardy* answer, but if it was, the question would be this: "What did George Washington say to his soldiers before they crossed the Delaware?" We share this interesting historic aside as our way of sounding the alarm, blowing the bugle, or whatever. It's time to move beyond preparation and practice and to leap into action. Walt Disney World here we come! Get in the boat, men!

Ready, Set, Tour!
Some Touring Considerations
HOW MUCH TIME IS REQUIRED
TO SEE EACH PARK?

The Magic Kingdom and Epcot offer such a large number of attractions and special live entertainment options that it is impossible to see everything in a single day, with or without a midday break. For a reasonably thorough tour of each, allocate a minimum of two days. The Animal Kingdom and the Disney-MGM Studios can be seen in a day, although planning on a day and a half allows for a more relaxed visit.

WHICH PARK TO SEE FIRST?

This question is less academic than it appears. Children who see the Magic Kingdom first expect more of the same type of entertainment at the other parks. At Epcot, children are often disappointed by the educational orientation and more serious tone (many adults react the same way). Disney-MGM offers some pretty wild action, but the general presentation is educational and more mature. Though most children enjoy zoos, live animals can't be programmed to entertain. Thus, children may not find the Animal Kingdom as exciting as the Magic Kingdom or Disney-MGM.

First-time visitors should see Epcot first; you will be able to enjoy it fully without having been preconditioned to think of Disney entertainment as solely fantasy or adventure. Children will be more likely to enjoy Epcot on its own merits if they see it first, and they will be more relaxed and patient in their touring.

See the Animal Kingdom second. Like Epcot, it has an educational thrust, but it provides a change of pace because it features live animals. Next, see Disney-MGM Studios, which helps all ages make a fluid transition from the educational Epcot and Animal Kingdom to the fanciful Magic Kingdom. Also, because Disney-MGM Studios is smaller, you won't walk as much or stay as long. Save the Magic Kingdom for last.

OPERATING HOURS

Disney can't be accused of being inflexible regarding operating hours at the parks. They run a dozen or more schedules each year, making it advisable to call (407) 824-4321 for the exact hours before you arrive. In the off-season, parks may be open for as few as eight hours (from 10 a.m. to 6 p.m.). By contrast, at busy times (particularly holidays), they may be open from 8 a.m. until 2 a.m. the next morning.

Usually, hours approximate the following: From September through mid-March, excluding holiday periods, the Magic Kingdom is open from 9 a.m. to 7, 8, or 9 p.m. During the same period, Epcot is open from 9 a.m. to 9 p.m., and Disney-MGM Studios is open from 9 a.m. to 7 or 8 p.m. The Animal Kingdom is open from 7 a.m. until 7 or 8 p.m. During summer, expect the Animal Kingdom to remain open until 8 p.m. Epcot and Disney-MGM Studios are normally open until 9 or 10 p.m., with the Magic Kingdom sometimes open as late as 1 a.m.

OFFICIAL OPENING VS. REAL OPENING

Operating hours you're quoted when you call are "official hours." The parks actually open earlier. Many visitors, relying on information disseminated by Disney Guest Relations, arrive at the official opening time and find the park packed with people. If the official hours are 9 a.m. to 9 p.m., for example, Main Street in the Magic Kingdom will open at 8 or 8:30 a.m. and the remainder of the park will open at 8:30 or 9 a.m. If the official opening for the Magic Kingdom is 8 a.m. and you're eligible for early entry (if you are staying in a Disney resort), you will be able to enter the park at 6:30 a.m.

Disney publishes hours of operation well in advance but allows the flexibility to react daily to gate conditions. Disney traffic controllers survey local hotel reservations, estimate how many visitors they should expect on a given day, and open the theme parks early to avoid bottlenecks at parking facilities and ticket windows and to absorb the crowds as they arrive.

If you don't have early-entry privileges, tour a park where early entry isn't in effect, arriving 50 minutes before the official opening time during the off-season. In midsummer arrive 70 minutes before official opening. If you visit on a major holiday, arrive one hour and 20 minutes before the official opening.

If you're a Disney resort guest and want to take advantage of early entry, arrive one hour and 40 minutes before the early-entry park is scheduled to open to the general public. Buses, boats, and monorails will initiate service to the early-entry park about two hours before it opens to the general public.

At day's end, rides and attractions shut down at approximately the official closing time. Main Street in the Magic Kingdom remains open 30 minutes to an hour after the rest of the park has closed.

THE RULES

Successful touring of the Magic Kingdom, the Animal Kingdom, Epcot, or Disney-MGM Studios hinges on five rules:

1. Determine in Advance What You Really Want to See

What rides and attractions appeal most to you? Which additional rides and attractions would you like to experience if you have some time left? What are you willing to forgo?

To help you set your touring priorities, we describe the theme parks and every attraction in detail in this book. In each description, we include the author's evaluation of the attraction and the opinions of Walt Disney World guests expressed as star ratings. Five stars is the best possible rating.

Finally, because attractions range from midway-type rides and horse-drawn trolleys to colossal, high-tech extravaganzas, we have developed a hierarchy of categories to pinpoint attractions' magnitude:

Super Headliners   The best attractions the theme park has to offer. Mind-boggling in size, scope, and imagination. Represents the cutting edge of modern attraction technology and design.

Headliners   Full blown, multimillion-dollar, full-scale themed adventures and theater presentations. Modern in technology and design and employing a full range of special effects.

Major Attractions   Themed adventures on a more modest scale, but incorporating state-of-the-art technologies. Or, larger-scale attractions of older design.

Minor Attractions   Midway-type rides, small "dark" rides (cars on a track, zigzagging through the dark), small theater presentations, transportation rides, and elaborate walk-through attractions.

Diversions   Exhibits, both passive and interactive. Includes playgrounds, video arcades, and street theater.

Though not every Walt Disney World attraction fits neatly into these descriptions, the categories provide a comparison of attraction size and scope. Remember that bigger and more elaborate doesn't always mean better. Peter Pan's Flight, a minor attraction in the Magic Kingdom, continues to be one of the park's most beloved rides. Likewise, for many young children, no attraction regardless of size surpasses Dumbo.

2. Arrive Early! Arrive Early! Arrive Early!

This is the single most important key to efficient touring and avoiding long lines. There are no lines and fewer people first thing in the morning. The same four rides you can experience in one hour in early morning can take as long as three hours to see after 10:30 a.m. Have breakfast before you arrive so you won't waste prime touring time sitting in a restaurant.

The earlier a park opens, the greater the potential advantage. This is because most vacationers won't make the sacrifice to rise early and get to a theme park before it opens. Fewer people are willing to be on hand for an 8 a.m. opening than for a 9 a.m. opening. On those rare occasions when a park opens at 10 a.m., almost everyone arrives at the same time, so it's almost impossible to get a jump on the crowd. If you're a Disney resort guest and have early-entry privileges, arrive as early as early entry allows (6:30 a.m. if the park opens to the public at 8 a.m., or 7:30 a.m. if the park opens to the public at 9 a.m.). If you are visiting during midsummer, arrive at non-early-entry parks 70 minutes before the official opening time. During holiday periods, arrive at non-early-entry parks 90 minutes to two hours before the official opening.

3. Avoid Bottlenecks

Crowd concentrations and/or faulty crowd management cause bottlenecks. Avoiding bottlenecks involves being able to predict where, when, and why they occur. Concentrations of hungry people create bottlenecks at restaurants during lunch and dinner. Concentrations of people moving toward the exit at closing time create bottlenecks in gift shops en route to the gate. Concentrations of visitors at new and popular rides and at rides slow to load and unload create bottlenecks and long lines. To help you get a grip on which attractions cause bottlenecks, we have developed a Bottleneck Scale with a range of one to ten. If an attraction ranks high on the Bottleneck Scale, try to experience it during the first two hours the park is open. The scale is included in each attraction profile in Parts 7 through 10.

4. Go Back to Your Hotel for a Rest in the Middle of the Day

You may think we're beating the dead horse with this midday nap thing, but if you plug away all day at the theme parks, you'll understand how the dead horse feels. No joke; resign yourself to going back to the hotel in the middle of the day for swimming, reading, and a snooze.

5. Let Off Steam

Time at a Disney theme park is extremely regimented for younger children. Often held close for fear of losing them, they are ushered from line to line and attraction to attraction throughout the day. After a couple of hours of being on such a short leash, it's not surprising that they're in need of some physical freedom and an opportunity to discharge that pent-up energy. As it happens, each of the major theme parks offers some sort of elaborate, creative playground perfect for such a release. At the Magic Kingdom it's Tom Sawyer Island, at the Animal Kingdom it's the Boneyard, and at the Disney-MGM Studios it's the "Honey, I Shrunk the Kids" Adventure Set. Epcot's play area, the Fitness Fairground in the Wonders of Life Pavilion is a little anemic in comparison to the other parks' playgrounds, but serves its purpose nonetheless. Be advised that each playground is fairly large, and it's pretty easy to misplace a child while they're exploring. All except the Fitness Fairgrounds, however, have only one exit, so although your kids might get lost within the playground, they cannot wonder off into the rest of the park without passing through the single exit (usually staffed by a Disney cast member).

YOUR DAILY ITINERARY

Plan each day in three blocks:

1. Early morning theme park touring
2. Midday break
3. Late afternoon and evening theme park touring

Choose the attractions that interest you most, and check their bottleneck ratings along with what time of day we recommend you visit. If your children are eight years old or younger, review the attraction's fright potential rating. Using the theme park maps in this guide, work out a step-by-step plan and write it down. Experience attractions with a high bottleneck rating as early as possible, transitioning to attractions with bottleneck ratings of six to eight around midmorning. Plan on departing the park for your midday break by 11:30 a.m. or so.

For your late afternoon and evening touring block, you do not necessarily have to return to the same theme park. If you have purchased one of the Disney admission options that allow you to "park hop," that is, visit more than one theme park on a given day, you may opt to spend the afternoon/evening block somewhere different. In any event, as you start your afternoon/evening block, see attractions with low bottleneck ratings until about 5 p.m. After 5 p.m., any attraction with a rating of one to seven is fair game. If you stay into the evening, try attractions with ratings of eight to ten during the hour just before closing.

In addition to the attractions, each theme park offers a broad range of special live entertainment events. We strongly recommend deferring these special parades, stage shows, and other productions until the afternoon/evening block. In the morning block, concentrate on the attractions. For the record, we regard live shows that offer five or more daily performances a day (except for street entertainment) as attractions. Thus, *Indiana Jones* at the Disney-MGM Studios is an attraction, as is *Festival of the Lion King* at the Animal Kingdom. *IllumiNations* at Epcot or the Main Street Electrical Parade at the Magic Kingdom, on the other hand, are live entertainment events. A schedule of live performances is listed on the handout park map available at the entrance of each park. When planning your day, also be aware that major live events draw large numbers of guests from the attraction lines. Thus, a good time to see an especially popular attraction is during a parade or other similar event.

VARIABLES THAT AFFECT HOW MUCH YOU'LL SEE

How quickly you move from one ride to another; when and how many refreshment and rest room breaks you take; when, where, and how you eat meals; and your ability (or lack thereof) to find your way around will all have an impact on how much you'll see. Smaller groups almost always move faster than larger groups, and families with older children and teens generally can cover more ground than families with young children. Switching off (see pages 124–126), among other things, prohibits families with little ones from moving expeditiously among attractions. Plus, some children simply cannot conform to the "arrive early!" rule.

A mom from Nutley, New Jersey, writes:

> *[Although you] advise getting to parks at opening, we just couldn't burn the candle at both ends. Our kids (10, 7, and 4) would not go to sleep early and couldn't be up at dawn and still stay relatively sane. It worked well for us to let them sleep a little later, go out and bring breakfast*

> *back to the room while they slept, and still get a relatively*
> *early start by not spending time on eating breakfast out.*
> *We managed to avoid long lines with an occasional early*
> *morning, and hitting popular attractions during parades,*
> *mealtimes, and late evenings.*

Finally, if you have young children in your party, be prepared for character encounters. The appearance of a Disney character is usually sufficient to stop your family dead in its tracks. What's more, although some characters continue to stroll the parks, it is becoming more the rule to assemble characters in some specific venue (like the Hall of Fame at Mickey's Toontown Fair) where families must line up for photos and autographs. Meeting characters, posing for photos, and collecting autographs can burn hours of touring time. If your kids are into character autograph collecting, you will need to anticipate these interruptions to your touring and negotiate some understanding with your children about when you will tour and when you will collect autographs. Our advice is to either go with the flow or alternatively set aside a certain morning or afternoon for photos and autographs. Be aware, however, that queues for autographs, especially in Toontown at the Magic Kingdom and Camp Minnie-Mickey at the Animal Kingdom, are every bit as long as the lines for major attractions. The only time-efficient way to collect autographs is to line up at the character greeting areas first thing in the morning. Because this is also the best time to experience the more popular attractions, you may have some tough decisions to make.

While we realize that starting early and going full-tilt through the morning might not be consistent with your idea of a vacation, it's still the best way to see the most popular attractions without long waits. We recommend, therefore, continuous, expeditious touring until around 11 a.m. or so. After that point, breaks and diversions won't affect your touring significantly.

Other variables that can profoundly affect your progress are beyond your control. Chief among these are the manner and timing of bringing a particular ride to capacity. For example, Big Thunder Mountain Railroad, a roller coaster in the Magic Kingdom, has five trains. On a given morning it may begin operation with two of the five, then add the other three if and when needed. If the waiting line builds rapidly before operators decide to go to full capacity, you could have a long wait, even in the early morning.

Another variable relates to the time you arrive for a theater performance. Usually, your wait will be the length of time from your arrival to the end of the presentation in progress. Thus, if Country Bear Jamboree is 15 minutes long and you arrive one minute after a show has begun, your wait for the next show will be 14 minutes. Conversely, if you arrive as the show is wrapping up, your wait will be only a minute or two.

A Word about Disney Thrill Rides

Readers of all ages should attempt to be open-minded about the so-called Disney "thrill rides." In comparison with rides at other theme parks, the Disney thrill attractions are quite tame, with more emphasis on sights, atmosphere, and special effects than on the motion, speed, or feel of the ride itself. While we suggest you take Disney's preride warnings seriously, we can tell you that guests of all ages report enjoying rides such as Tower of Terror, Big Thunder Mountain, and Splash Mountain.

A reader from Washington sums up the situation well:

> Our boys and I are used to imagining typical amusement park rides when it comes to roller coasters. So, when we thought of Big Thunder Mountain and Space Mountain, what came to mind was gigantic hills, upside down loops, huge vertical drops, etc. I actually hate roller coasters, especially the unpleasant sensation of a long drop, and I have never taken a ride that loops you upside down.
>
> In fact, the Disney [thrill rides] are all tame in comparison. There are never any long and steep hills (except Splash Mountain, and it is there for anyone to see, so you have informed consent going on the ride). I was able to build up courage to go on all of them, and the more I rode them the more I enjoyed them—the less you tense up expecting a big long drop, the more you enjoy the special effects and even swinging around curves. Swinging around curves is really the primary motion challenge of Disney roller coasters.

Disney, recognizing that it needs more attractions that appeal to the youth and young adult markets, is in the process of adding some roller coasters to its parks. The new Rock 'n' Roller Coaster at the Disney-MGM Studios will incorporate at least some of the features our Washington reader seeks to avoid.

A WORD ABOUT HEIGHT REQUIREMENTS

A number of attractions require children to meet minimum height and age requirements, usually 44 inches tall to ride with an adult, or 44 inches and 7 years of age to ride alone. If you have children too short or too young to ride, you have several options, including switching off (described on pages 124–126). Although the alternatives may resolve some practical and logistic issues, be forewarned that your smaller children might nonetheless be resentful of their older (or taller) siblings who qualify to ride. A mom from Virginia bumped into just such a situation, writing:

> *You mention height requirements for rides but not the intense sibling jealousy this can generate. Frontierland was a real problem in that respect. Our very petite 5 year old, to her outrage, was stuck hanging around while our 8-year old went on Splash Mountain and [Big] Thunder Mountain with Grandma and Grandad, and the nearby alternatives weren't helpful [too long a line for rafts to Tom Sawyer Island, etc.]. If we had thought ahead, we would have left the younger kid back in Mickey's Toontown with one of the grownups for another roller coaster ride or two and then met up later at a designated point. The best areas had a playground or other quick attractions for short people near the rides with height requirements, like the Boneyard near the dinosaur ride [Countdown To extinction] at the Animal Kingdom.*

The reader makes a valid point, though in practical terms splitting the group and then meeting later can be more complicated that she might imagine. If you choose to split up, ask the Disney greeter at the entrance to the attraction(s) with height requirements how long the wait is. If you tack five minutes for riding onto the anticipated wait, and then add five or so minutes to exit and reach the meeting point, you'll have an approximate sense of how long the younger kids (and their supervising adult) will have to do other stuff. Our guess is that even with a long line for the rafts, the reader would have had more than sufficient time to take her daughter to Tom Sawyer Island while the sibs rode Splash Mountain and Big Thunder Mountain with the grandparents. For sure she had time to tour the Swiss Family Treehouse in adjacent Adventureland.

WAITING LINE STRATEGIES FOR ADULTS WITH YOUNG CHILDREN

Children hold up better through the day if you minimize the time they spend in lines. Arriving early and using our touring plans immensely reduces waiting. Here are additional ways to reduce stress for children:

1. Line Games   Wise parents anticipate restlessness in line and plan activities to reduce the stress and boredom. In the morning, have waiting children discuss what they want to see and do during the day. Later, watch for and count Disney characters or play simple guessing games like 20 Questions. Lines move continuously, so games requiring pen and paper are impractical. Waiting in the holding area of a theater attraction, however, is a different story. Here, tic-tac-toe, hangman, drawing, and coloring make the time fly by.

2. Last-Minute Entry   If an attraction can accommodate an unusually large number of people at once, it's often unnecessary to stand in line. The Magic Kingdom's *Liberty Belle* Riverboat is a good example. The boat holds about 450 people, usually more than are waiting in line. Instead of standing uncomfortably in a crowd, grab a snack and sit in the shade until the boat arrives and loading is under way. After the line is almost gone, join it.

At large-capacity theaters like that for Epcot's *The American Adventure,* ask the entrance greeter how long it will be until guests are admitted for the next show. If it's 15 minutes or more, take a rest room break or get a snack, returning a few minutes before the show starts. You aren't allowed to carry food or drink into the attraction, so make sure you have time to finish your snack before entering.

Attractions You Can Usually Enter at the Last Minute

Magic Kingdom

Liberty Square

The Hall of Presidents
Liberty Belle Riverboat

Tomorrowland

The Timekeeper

Epcot

Future World

The Circle of Life
(except during mealtimes)
Food Rocks
(except during mealtimes)

World Showcase

Wonders of China
The American Adventure
O Canada!

Disney-MGM Studios

Doug Live

3. The Hail Mary Pass   Certain lines are configured to allow you and your smaller children to pass under the rail to join your partner just before actual boarding or entry. This technique allows children and one adult to rest, snack, cool off, or go potty while another adult or older sibling stands in line. Other guests are very understanding about this strategy when used for young children. You're likely to meet hostile opposition, however, if you try to pass older children or more than one adult under the rail. The best way to preempt hostility is to tell the folks behind you in line exactly what you are doing and why.

Attractions Where You Can Usually Complete a Hail Mary Pass

Magic Kingdom

Adventureland

Swiss Family Treehouse
Jungle Cruise

Frontierland

Country Bear Jamboree

Attractions Where You Can Usually Complete a Hail Mary Pass (continued)	
Fantasyland	Mad Tea Party Snow White's Adventures Dumbo the Flying Elephant Cinderella's Golden Carrousel Peter Pan's Flight
Tomorrowland	Tomorrowland Speedway
Epcot	
Future World	Spaceship Earth Living with the Land
Disney-MGM Studios	Sounds Dangerous Indiana Jones Epic Stunt Spectacular!

4. Switching Off (a.k.a. The Baby Swap)   Several attractions have minimum height and/or age requirements, usually 3'8" tall to ride with an adult, or age 7 *and* 3'8" to ride alone. Some couples with children too small or too young forgo these attractions, while others take turns to ride. Missing some of Disney's best rides is an unnecessary sacrifice, and waiting in line twice for the same ride is a tremendous waste of time.

Instead, take advantage of the "switching off" option, also called "The Baby Swap." To switch off, there must be at least two adults. Everybody waits in line together, adults and children. When you reach an attendant (called a "greeter"), tell him or her that you want to switch off. The greeter will allow everyone, including the young children, to enter the attraction. When you reach the loading area, one adult rides while the other stays with the kids. Then the riding adult disembarks and takes charge of the children while the other adult rides. A third adult in the party can ride twice, once with each of the switching off adults, so that the switching off adults don't have to experience the attraction alone.

Most rides with age and height minimums load and unload in the same area, facilitating switching off. An exception is Space

Switching Off

Mountain, where the first adult at the conclusion of the ride must also inform the unloading attendant that he or she is switching off. The attendant will admit the first adult to an internal stairway that goes back to the loading area.

Attractions at which switching off is practiced are oriented to more mature guests. Sometimes it takes a lot of courage for a child just to move through the queue holding dad's hand. In the boarding area, many children suddenly fear abandonment as one parent leaves to experience the attraction. Unless your children are prepared for switching off, you might have an emotional crisis on your hands. A mom from Edison, New Jersey, advises:

> Once my son came to understand that the switch-off would not leave him abandoned, he did not seem to mind. I would recommend to your readers that they practice the switch-off on some dry runs at home, so that their child is not concerned that he will be left behind. At the very least, the procedure could be explained in advance so that the little ones know what to expect.

Finally, a mother from Ada, Michigan, who discovered that the procedure for switching off varies from attraction to attraction, offered this suggestion:

> Parents need to tell the very first attendant they come to that they would like to switch off. Each attraction has a different procedure for this. Tell every other attendant too because they forget quickly.

Attractions Where Switching Off Is Common	
Magic Kingdom	
Tomorrowland	Space Mountain
	Alien Encounter
Frontierland	Splash Mountain
	Big Thunder Mountain Railroad
Epcot	
Future World	Body Wars
	Test Track

Attractions Where Switching Off Is Common (continued)	
Disney-MGM Studios	Star Tours
	The Twilight Zone Tower of Terror
	Rock 'n' Roller Coaster
Animal Kingdom	
DinoLand U.S.A.	Countdown to Extinction
Asia	Kali River Rapids

5. How to Ride Twice in a Row without Waiting Many young children like to ride a favorite attraction two or more times in succession. Riding the second time often gives them a feeling of mastery and accomplishment. Unfortunately, even in the early morning, repeat rides can be time consuming. If you ride Dumbo as soon as the Magic Kingdom opens, for instance, you will wait only a minute or two for your first ride. When you come back for your second, the wait will be about 12 minutes. If you want to ride a third time, count on 20 minutes or longer.

The best way to get your child on the ride twice (or more) without blowing your morning is to use the "Chuck Bubba Relay" (named in honor of a Kentucky reader):

a. Mom and little Bubba enter the waiting line.

b. Dad lets a specific number of people go in front of him (24 at Dumbo), then gets in line.

c. As soon as the ride stops, mom exits with Bubba and passes him to dad to ride the second time.

d. If everybody is really getting into this, mom can hop in line again, no fewer than 24 people behind dad.

The Chuck Bubba Relay won't work on every ride, because waiting areas are configured differently (that is, it's impossible in some cases to exit the ride and make the pass). For those rides (all in Fantasyland) where the Bubba Relay works, here are the numbers of people to count off:

Mad Tea Party: 53
Snow White's Adventures: 52
Dumbo the Flying Elephant: 24
Cinderella's Golden Carrousel: 75
Peter Pan's Flight: 64

If you're the second adult in the relay, you'll reach a place in line where it's easiest to make the hand-off. This may be where those exiting the ride pass closest to those waiting to board. In any event, you'll know it when you see it. If you reach it and the first parent hasn't arrived with Bubba, let those behind you pass until Bubba shows up.

6. Last-Minute Cold Feet   If your young child gets cold feet just before boarding a ride where there is no age or height requirement, you usually can arrange with the loading attendant for a switch off. This is common at Pirates of the Caribbean, where children lose their courage while winding through the dungeon-like waiting area. Additionally, no law says you *have* to ride. If you reach the boarding area and someone is unhappy, tell an attendant you've changed your mind and you'll be shown the way out.

7. Elevator Shoes for the Short and the Brave   If you have a child who is begging to go on the rides with height requirements but who is a little too short, slip heel lifts into his Nikes before he reaches the measuring point. Be sure to leave the heel lifts in, because he may be measured again before boarding.

A Huntsville, Alabama, mom has worked out all the details on the heel lift problem:

> *Knowing my wild child 3-year-old as I do, I was inter-ested in your comment regarding shoe lifts. I don't know about other places, but in the big city of Huntspatch where we live, one has to have a prescription for lifts. Normal shoe repair places don't make them. I couldn't think of a material with which to fashion a homemade lift that would be comfortable enough to stand on while waiting in line. I ended up purchasing some of those painfully ugly 2-inch chunky-heeled sandals at my local 'mart where they carried these hideous shoes in unbeliev-ably tiny sizes ($12). Since they didn't look too comfort-*

able, we popped them on her right before we entered the ride lines. None of the height checkers ever asked her to remove them and she clip clopped onto Splash Mountain, Big Thunder Railroad (Dat BIG Choo-Choo), Star Wars, and The Tower of Terror - twice! However, the same child became so terrified at the Tiki Bird show that we were forced to leave - go figure! For adventuresome boys, I would suggest purchasing some of those equally hideous giant-heeled cowboy boots.

Disney World Problem 204: Too Short to Ride

Along similar lines, a Long Pond, Pennsylvania, mom had this to offer:

> *Tower of Terror, Star Tours & Body Wars are 40"*
> *requirements. Being persistent with a 39-1/2" child, we*
> *tried these several times. She got on Tower of Terror 2 of*
> *3 times, Body Wars 1 of 1 time, & Star Tours 1 of 2*
> *tries. She wore elevator shoes & a bun hair style to*
> *increase height.*

8. Catch-22 at Tomorrowland Speedway   Though Tomorrowland Speedway is a great treat for young children, they're required to be 4'4" tall in order to drive. Few children age six and younger measure up, so the ride is essentially withheld from the very age group that would most enjoy it. To resolve this catch-22, go on the ride with your small child. The attendants will assume that you will drive. After getting into the car, shift your child over behind the steering wheel. From your position, you will still be able to control the foot pedals. Children will feel like they're really driving, and because the car travels on a self-guiding track, there's no way they can make a mistake while steering.

9. Astro Orbiter—A Safety Warning   Parents often board the rocket before lifting their child aboard. Because the attendant can't see small children beside the vehicle from his control station, the ride may start before a child is safely in the cockpit. If you take a small child on this ride, put the child in the rocket first, then get in.

Character Analysis

The large and friendly costumed versions of Mickey, Minnie, Donald, Goofy, and others—known as "Disney characters"—provide a link between Disney animated films and the theme parks. To people emotionally invested, the characters in Disney films are as real as next-door neighbors, never mind that they're just drawings on plastic. In recent years, theme park personifications of the characters also have become real to us. It's not just a person in a mouse costume they see; it is Mickey himself. Similarly, meeting Goofy or Snow White in Fantasyland is an encounter with a celebrity, a memory to be treasured.

While there are hundreds of Disney animated film characters, only about 250 have been brought to life in costume. Of these, a relatively small number (less than a fifth) are "greeters" (characters who mix with patrons). The remaining characters perform in shows or parades. Originally confined to the Magic Kingdom, characters are now found in all the major theme parks and Disney hotels.

Character Watching   Character watching has become a pastime. Families once were content to meet characters only occasionally and by chance. They now pursue them relentlessly, armed with autograph books and cameras. Because some characters are only rarely seen, character watching has become character collecting. (To cash in on character collecting, Disney sells autograph books throughout the World.) Mickey, Minnie, and Goofy are a snap to bag; they seem to be everywhere. But Winnie the Pooh seldom comes out. Other characters appear regularly, but only in a location consistent with their starring role. Cinderella, predictably, reigns at Cinderella Castle in Fantasyland, while Brer Fox and Brer Bear frolic in Frontierland near Splash Mountain.

A dad from Brooklyn thinks the character autograph–hunting craze has gotten out of hand, complaining:

> *Whoever started the practice of collecting autographs from the characters should be subjected to Chinese water torture! We went to WDW 11 years ago, with an eight-year-old and an eleven-year-old. We would bump into characters, take pictures, and that was it. After a while, our children noticed that some of the other children were getting autographs. We managed to avoid joining in during our first day at the Magic Kingdom and our first day at Epcot, but by day three our children were collecting autographs. However, it did not get too out of hand, since it was limited to accidental character meeting.*

This year when we took our youngest child (who is now age eight), he had already seen his siblings' collection, and was determined to outdo them. However, rather than random meetings, the characters are now available practically all day long at different locations, according to a printed schedule, which our son was old enough to read. We spent more time standing in line for auto-graphs than we did for the most popular rides!

A family from Birmingham, Alabama, found some benefit in their children's relentless pursuit of characters, writing:

> We had no idea we would be caught up in this madness, but after my daughters grabbed your guidebook to get Poc-ahontas to sign it (we had no blank paper), we quickly bought a Disney autograph book and gave in. It was actually the highlight of their trip, and my son even got into the act by helping get places in line for his sisters. They LOVED looking for characters (I think it has all been planned by Kodak to sell film). The possibility of see-ing a new character revived my seven-year-old's energy on many occasions. It was an amazing totally unexpected part of our visit.

Finding Mickey   Many children expect to meet Mickey the minute they enter the park and are disappointed when he isn't around. If your children can't enjoy things until they see Mickey, ask a cast member where to find him. If the cast member doesn't know right away, he or she can find out quickly. Cast members have a number they can call to learn exactly where the characters are at any time.

"Then Some Confusion Happened"   Young children some-times become lost at character encounters. Usually, there's a lot of activity around a character, with both adults and children touching it or posing for pictures. Most commonly, mom and dad stay in the crowd while Junior approaches to meet the char-acter. In the excitement and with people milling and the charac-ter moving around, Junior heads off in the wrong direction to look for mom and dad. In the words of a Salt Lake City mom: "Milo was shaking hands with Dopey one minute, then some confusion happened and [Milo] was gone."

Families with several young children and parents who are busy with cameras can lose track of a youngster in a heartbeat. Our recommendation for parents with preschoolers is to stay with the kids when they meet characters, stepping back only to take a quick picture.

MEETING CHARACTERS FOR FREE

You can *see* Disney characters in live shows at all the theme parks and in parades at the Magic Kingdom and Disney-MGM Studios. Consult your daily entertainment schedule for times. If you want to *meet* the characters, get autographs, and take photos, pick up a copy of the *Disney Character Greeting Location Guide,* available free at each park.

At the Magic Kingdom   Characters are encountered more frequently here than anywhere else in Walt Disney World. There almost always will be a character next to City Hall on Main Street and usually one or more in Town Square or near the railroad station. If it's rainy, look for characters on the veranda of Tony's Town Square Restaurant. Characters appear in all the lands but are more plentiful in Fantasyland and Mickey's Toontown Fair. At Mickey's Toontown Fair, you can meet Mickey privately in his Judge's Tent. Characters actually work shifts at the Toontown Hall of Fame next to Mickey's Country House. Here, you can line up to meet three different assortments of characters. Each assortment has its own greeting area and, of course, its own line. One group, variously labeled Mickey's Pals or Famous Friends or something similar, will include Minnie, Pluto, Goofy, Donald, and sometimes Chip 'n' Dale, Daisy, and Uncle Scrooge. The other two assortments vary and are more ambiguously defined. The 100 Acre Wood Friends are mostly Winnie the Pooh characters, while Fairy Tale Friends include Snow White, assorted dwarfs, Sleeping Beauty, the Beast, Belle, Cinderella, Prince Charming, and so on. Sometimes, however, it's Villains (Captain Hook, Cruella DeVil, Jabar, et al.) and Princesses (Sleeping Beauty, Mary Poppins, yadda, yadda, yadda). Cinderella regularly greets diners at Cinderella's Royal Table in the castle. Also look for characters in the central hub and by Splash Mountain in Frontierland.

Characters are featured in afternoon and evening parades and also play a major role in Castle Forecourt shows (at the entrance to the castle on the moat side) and at the Galaxy Palace Theater in Tomorrowland. Find performance times for shows and parades in the park's daily entertainment schedule. Sometimes characters stay to greet the audience after shows.

At Epcot   At first Disney didn't think characters would be appropriate for the more serious, educational style of Epcot. Later, in response to criticism that Epcot lacked warmth and humor, characters were imported. To integrate them thematically, new and often bizarre costumes were created. Goofy roams Future World in a metallic silver cape reminiscent of Buck Rogers. Mickey greets guests at the American Adventure dressed like Ben Franklin.

It's unclear whether there are fewer characters at Epcot or if it just seems that way because the place is so big. In any event, don't expect to encounter either the number or variety of characters at Epcot that you would in the Magic Kingdom. Two Epcot original characters, Dreamfinder and Figment, are found at the Journey into Imagination pavilion in Future World, and assorted characters appear at the Showcase Plaza each morning. Characters are also occasionally found at the American Adventure pavilion and at the United Kingdom in World Showcase. Characters aren't featured in parades at Epcot, but character shows are performed daily at the American Gardens Theater in World Showcase. Check the park's daily entertainment schedule.

Characters may be rarer at Epcot, but they're often easier to meet. A father from Effingham, Illinois, writes:

> *Trying to get autographs and pictures with Disney characters in the Magic Kingdom was a nightmare. Every character we saw was mobbed by kids and adults. Our kids had no chance. But at Epcot and Disney-MGM, things were much better. We got autographs, pictures, and more involvement. Our kids danced with several characters and received a lot of personal attention.*

At Disney-MGM Studios   Characters are likely to turn up anywhere at the Studios but are most frequently found in front of the Animation Building, along Mickey Avenue (leading to the soundstages), and at the end of New York Street on the backlot. Mickey and his "friends" pose for keepsake photos (about $10 each) on Hollywood Boulevard, Sunset Boulevard, and New York Street. Characters are also prominent in shows, with *Voyage of the Little Mermaid* running almost continuously and an abbreviated version of *Beauty and the Beast* performed several times daily at the Theater of the Stars. Check the daily entertainment schedule for show times.

At the Animal Kingdom   Camp Minnie-Mickey in the Animal Kingdom is a special location designed specifically for meeting characters. There are four designated character greeting "trails" where you can meet Mickey, Minnie, and various characters from *The Jungle Book* and *The Lion King*. Also at Camp Minnie-Mickey are two stage shows featuring characters from *The Lion King* and *Pocahontas.*

Responding to requests, each theme park has added a lot of information about characters to its handout map. The reverse side lists where and when certain characters will be available and provides information on character dining. As mentioned earlier, a handout devoted exclusively to character watching, the *Disney Character Greeting Location Guide,* is now commonly available at all of the theme parks except the Animal Kingdom.

Disney has taken several initiatives intended to satisfy guests' inexhaustible desire to meet the characters. Most important, Disney assigned Mickey and a number of other characters to all-day duty in Mickey's Toontown Fair in the Magic Kingdom and Camp Minnie-Mickey in the Animal Kingdom. Although making the characters more available has taken the guesswork out of finding them, it has robbed encounters of much of their spontaneity. Instead of chancing on a character, it's much more common now to wait in line to meet the character. Speaking of which, be aware that lines for face characters move m-u-c-h more slowly than do lines for nonspeaking characters. Because face characters are allowed to talk, they often engage children in lengthy conversations, much to the dismay of families still in the queue.

Dining

For efficiency and economy, we recommend eating breakfast in your hotel room. Even if you roll out to Denny's or eat breakfast at your hotel, however, finish early enough to arrive at the theme park prior to opening. For lunch it's cheaper and more relaxed to eat out of the parks during your midday break. If you elect not to take a midday break, you won't have any trouble finding something your children will eat. Hamburgers, fries, hot dogs, or pizza can be had within 50 yards of any attraction. Plan on spending about twice what you would pay at a Hardee's or McDonald's.

For a counter-service lunch or dinner, we suggest the following eateries:

Magic Kingdom
Aunt Polly's Dockside Inn
Columbia Harbour House
Diamond Horseshoe
   Saloon
The Plaza Pavilion

Disney-MGM Studios
ABC Commissary
Backlot Express
Toy Story Pizza Planet

Animal Kingdom
Flame Tree Barbecue
Pizzafari
Tuskers House Restaurant

Epcot
Electric Umbrella
   Restaurant
Pasta Piazza Ristorante
Pure and Simple
Sommerfest
Yakitori House

No matter how formal or imposing a Disney full-service restaurant appears, rest assured that the staff is accustomed to wiggling, impatient, and often boisterous children. Bottom line: Young children are the rule, not the exception, at Disney restaurants. Almost all Disney restaurants offer a child's menu, and all have booster seats and high chairs. Because the wait staff understands how tough it can be for children to sit still for an extended period, they will supply your little ones with crackers and rolls and serve your dinner much faster than in comparable restaurants elsewhere. And if your children raise the roof? No problem, the other diners will be too preoccupied with their own kids to notice.

CHARACTER DINING

Fraternizing with characters has become so popular that Disney offers character breakfasts, brunches, and dinners where families can dine in the presence of Mickey, Minnie, Goofy, and other costumed versions of animated celebrities. Besides grabbing customers from Denny's and Hardee's, character meals provide a familiar, controlled setting in which young children can warm gradually to characters. Though we mention only the featured character(s) in the following descriptions, all meals are attended by several characters. Adult prices apply to persons age 12 or older, children's prices to ages 3 to 11. Little ones under age 3 eat free. For additional information on character dining, call (407) 939-3463 (WDW-DINE).

Because character dining is very popular, we recommend that you arrange priority seating as far in advance as possible. Make priority seating for dining up to 60 days before arrival by calling (407) 939-3463. If you forget to arrange priority seating in advance and all resort and theme park character meals are sold out, try to book a character meal at the Swan or Dolphin. Because the Swan and Dolphin aren't Disney-owned hotels, their character meals aren't booked through Disney central reservations. Consequently, the Swan and Dolphin often will have seating available when all other character meals are booked.

Priority seating is not a reservation, only a commitment to seat you ahead of walk-in patrons at the scheduled date and time. A reserved table won't await you, but you will be seated ahead of patrons who failed to call ahead. Even with priority seating, expect to wait at least 30 minutes to be seated.

Character Dining: What to Expect

Character meals are bustling affairs, held in hotels' or theme parks' largest full-service restaurants. Character breakfasts offer a buffet or a fixed menu served family-style. The typical family-style breakfast includes scrambled eggs; bacon, sausage, and ham; hash browns; waffles or French toast; biscuits, rolls, or pastries; and fruit. The meal is served in large skillets or platters at your table. If you run out of something, you can order seconds (or thirds) at no additional charge. Buffets offer much the same fare, but you have to fetch it yourself.

Character dinners range from a set menu served family-style to buffets or ordering off the menu. The character dinner at the Liberty Tree Tavern in the Magic Kingdom, for example, is served family-style and consists of turkey, ham, marinated flank steak, salad, mashed potatoes, green vegetables, and, for kids, macaroni and cheese. Dessert is extra. Character dinner buffets, such as those at 1900 Park Fare at the Grand Floridian and Chef Mickey's at the Contemporary Resort, offer separate adults' and children's serving lines. Typically, the children's buffet includes hamburgers, hot dogs, pizza, fish sticks, fried chicken nuggets, macaroni and cheese, and peanut butter and jelly sandwiches. Selections at the adult buffet usually include prime rib or other carved meat, baked or broiled Florida seafood, pasta, chicken, an ethnic dish or two, vegetables, potatoes, and salad.

At both breakfasts and dinners, characters circulate around the room while you eat. During your meal, each of the three to five characters present will visit your table, arriving one at a time to cuddle the kids (and sometimes the adults), pose for photos, and sign autographs. Keep autograph books (with pens) and loaded cameras handy. For the best photos, adults should sit across the table from their children. Always seat the children where characters can reach them most easily. If a table is against a wall, for example, adults should sit with their backs to the wall and children on the aisle.

At some of the larger restaurants, including 'Ohana at the Polynesian Resort and Chef Mickey's at the Contemporary, character meals involve impromptu parades of characters and children around the room, group singing, napkin waving, and other organized mayhem.

Disney people don't rush you to leave after you've eaten. You can get seconds on coffee or juice and stay as long as you wish to enjoy the characters. Remember, however, that there are lots of eager children and adults waiting not so patiently to be admitted.

When to Go

Though a number of character breakfasts are offered around Walt Disney World, attending them usually prevents you from arriving at the theme parks in time for opening. Because early morning is best for touring the parks and you don't want to burn daylight lingering over breakfast, we suggest:

1. Substitute a character breakfast for lunch. Have juice or coffee and a roll or banana from room service or from your cooler first thing in the morning to tide you over. Then tour the theme park for an hour or two before breaking off around 10:15 a.m. to go to the character breakfast of your choice. Make a big brunch of your character breakfast and skip lunch. You should be fueled until dinner.

2. Go on your arrival or departure day. The day you arrive and check in is usually good for a character dinner. Settle in at your hotel, swim, then dine with the characters.

This strategy has the added benefit of exposing your children to the characters before chance encounters at the parks. Some children, moreover, won't settle down to enjoy the parks until they have seen Mickey. Departure days also are good for a character meal. Schedule a character breakfast on your check-out day before you head for the airport or begin your drive home.

3. Go on a rest day. If you plan to stay five or more days, you probably will take a day or a half-day from touring to rest or do something else. These are perfect days for a character meal.

4. Go for dinner instead of breakfast. A character dinner in late afternoon or evening won't conflict with your touring schedule.

Character Breakfasts

If your kids are picky eaters or simply don't like eggs, choose a buffet breakfast. Priority seating is recommended for all character breakfasts. Call (407) 939-3463 for breakfasts at Disney resorts or in theme parks. For non-Disney hotels, call the hotel directly.

Character Campfire

A campfire and sing-along are held nightly at 7 or 8 p.m. (depending on the season) near the Meadow Trading Post and Bike Barn at Fort Wilderness Campground. Chip 'n' Dale lead the songs, and a full-length Disney film is shown afterward. The program is free and open to resort guests. For a schedule, call (407) 824-2788.

Strollers

Strollers are available for a modest daily rental fee at all four major theme parks. If you rent a stroller at the Magic Kingdom and decide to go to Epcot, the Animal Kingdom, or Disney-MGM Studios, turn in your Magic Kingdom stroller and keep your receipt to present at the next park. You'll be issued another stroller without additional charge.

Strollers at the Magic Kingdom, the Animal Kingdom, and Epcot are large, sturdy models with sun canopies. We have seen families load as many as three children at once in one of these. Strollers at Disney-MGM Studios are the light, collapsible type. Strollers can be obtained to the right of the entrance at the Magic Kingdom, to the left of the Entrance Plaza at Epcot, and at Oscar's Super Service just inside the entrance of Disney-MGM Studios. Stroller rentals at the Animal Kingdom are just inside the entrance and to the right. Rental at all parks is fast and efficient, and returning the stroller is a breeze. Even at Epcot, where as many as 900 strollers are turned in after the evening fireworks, there's almost no wait or hassle. If you don't mind forfeiting your dollar deposit, you can ditch your rental stroller anywhere in the park when you're ready to leave.

When you enter a show or board a ride, you must park your stroller, usually in an open, unprotected area. If it rains before you return, you'll need a cloth, towel, or diaper to dry it.

Strollers are a must for infants and toddlers, but we have observed many sharp parents renting strollers for somewhat older children (up to five years old or so). The stroller prevents parents from having to carry children when they sag and provides a convenient place to carry water and snacks.

If you go to your hotel for a break and intend to return to the park, leave your rental stroller by an attraction near the entrance, marking it with something personal like a bandanna. When you return after your break, your stroller will be waiting for you.

Also, be aware that rental strollers are too large for all infants and many toddlers. If you plan to rent a stroller for your infant or toddler, bring along some pillows, cushions, or rolled towels for baby buttressing.

It's permissible to bring your own stroller from home. Remember, however, that only collapsible strollers are permitted on monorails and buses. Your stroller is unlikely to be stolen, but mark it clearly with your name.

We should report that an increasing number of reader complaints are being directed at Disney's rental strollers. The following are representative:

A mother from Williamsville, New York didn't think much of the rental strollers at the Magic Kingdom and Epcot:

> *My biggest complaint about the parks, and I would find it hard to believe if no one has mentioned this to you yet,*

*concerns those antiquated strollers used at MK and Epcot.
Those things are metal and vinyl monstrosities. Needless to
say, the metal pieces had the tendency to become hot and
the vinyl was sticky. Also, these little vehicles had no
brakes which, at times, made them difficult to get in and
out of safely. Aside from these safety issues, which are reason enough for Disney to spring for newer models, the
strollers alone date the park much more than Tomorrowland ever did.*

A Canton, Ohio dad agreed, writing:

*The strollers at the parks leave a lot to be desired. The
strollers at the Animal Kingdom are by far the best, with
adequate room for small children and good maneuver-
ability. The strollers at MGM Studios have adequate
room but are difficult to maneuver. The strollers at
EPCOT and the Magic Kingdom are old, too small except
for very young children and not very easy to maneuver
(my five year old daughter had to sit with her legs hanging out of the stroller because it was so small).*

Sometimes strollers disappear while you're enjoying a ride or
show. Disney cast members often rearrange strollers parked outside an attraction. Sometimes this is done to "tidy up." At other
times, strollers are moved to clear a walkway. Don't assume your
stroller has been stolen because it isn't where you left it. It may
be "neatly arranged" a few feet away.

Sometimes, however, rental strollers are taken by mistake or
ripped off by people not wanting to spend time replacing one that's
missing. Don't be alarmed if yours disappears. You won't have to
buy the missing stroller, and you'll be issued a new one for your con-
tinued use. In the Magic Kingdom, replacements are available at
Tinker Bell's Treasures in Fantasyland, at Merchant of Venus in
Tomorrowland, and at the main rental facility near the park entrance.
At Epcot, get replacements at the Entrance Plaza rental headquarters and at the International Gateway (in World Showcase between
the United Kingdom and France). Strollers at Disney-MGM can
be replaced at Oscar's Super Service and at Endor Vendors near Star
Tours. In the Animal Kingdom, stroller replacements are available
at Garden Gate Gifts and Mombasa Marketplace.

Replacing a stroller is no big deal, but it's inconvenient. A family from Minnesota complained that their stroller had been taken six times in one day at Epcot and five times in a day at Disney-MGM Studios. Even with free replacements, larceny on this scale certainly represents a lot of wasted time. Through our own experiments and readers' suggestions, we have developed techniques for hanging on to a rented stroller: Affix something personal (but expendable) to the handle. Evidently, most strollers are pirated by mistake (they all look alike) or because it's easier to swipe someone else's stroller than to replace one when it disappears. Since most stroller "theft" results from confusion or laziness, the average pram pincher will hesitate to haul off a stroller bearing another person's property.

Lastly, you would be amazed at how many people are injured by strollers pushed by parents who are driving aggressively, in a hurry, or in the ozone. Though you may desire to use your stroller as a battering ram or to wedge through crowds like Moses parting the seas, think twice. It's very un-Disney to steamroll other guests.

When Kids Get Lost

If one of your children gets separated from you, don't panic. All things considered, Walt Disney World is about the safest place to get lost we can think of. Disney cast members are trained to watch for seemingly lost kids, and because children become detached from parents so frequently in the theme parks, cast members know exactly what to do.

If you lose a child in the Magic Kingdom, report it to a Disney employee, then check at the Baby Center and at City Hall where lost-children "logs" are kept. At Epcot, report the loss, then check at Baby Services near the Odyssey Center. At Disney-MGM Studios, report the situation at the Guest Relations Building at the entrance end of Hollywood Boulevard. At Animal Kingdom, go to the Baby Center in Safari Village. Paging isn't used, but in an emergency an "all points bulletin" can be issued throughout the park(s) via internal communications. If a Disney employee encounters a lost child, he or she will immediately take the child to the park's guest relations center or its baby-care center.

As comforting as this knowledge is, however, it's nevertheless scary when a child turns up missing. Fortunately, circumstances surrounding a child becoming lost are fairly predictable and, for the most part, preventable.

For starters, consider how much alike children dress, especially in warm climates where shorts and T-shirts are the norm. Throw your children in with 10,000 other kids the same size and suddenly that "cute little outfit" turns into theme park camouflage. We suggest that children younger than age eight be color-coded by dressing them in "vacation uniforms" with distinctively colored T-shirts or equally eye-catching apparel. It's also smart to sew a label into each child's shirt that states his or her name, your family name, your hometown, and the name of your hotel. The same thing can be accomplished by writing the information on a strip of masking tape. Hotel security professionals suggest the information be printed in small letters and the tape be affixed to the outside of the child's shirt, five inches below the armpit. Also, special name tags can be obtained at the major theme parks.

Other than just blending in, children tend to become separated from their parents under remarkably similar circumstances:

1. Preoccupied Solo Parent   In this situation, the party's only adult is preoccupied with something like buying refreshments, loading the camera, or using the rest room. Junior is there one second and gone the next.

2. The Hidden Exit   Sometimes parents wait on the sidelines while two or more young children experience a ride together. Parents expect the kids to exit in one place and, lo and behold, the youngsters pop out somewhere else. Exits from some attractions are distant from the entrances. Make sure you know exactly where your children will emerge before letting them ride by themselves.

3. After the Show   At the end of many shows and rides, a Disney staffer will announce, "Check for personal belongings and take small children by the hand." When dozens, if not hundreds, of people leave an attraction simultaneously, it's surprisingly easy for parents to lose contact with their children unless they have them directly in tow.

4. Rest Room Problems   Mom tells six-year-old Tommy, "I'll be sitting on this bench when you come out of the rest room." Three possibilities: One, Tommy exits through a different door and becomes disoriented (Mom may not know there *is* another door). Two, Mom decides she also will use the rest room, and Tommy emerges to find her gone. Three, Mom pokes around in a shop while keeping an eye on the bench, but misses Tommy when he comes out.

If you can't be with your child in the rest room, make sure there's only one exit. The rest room on a passageway between Frontierland and Adventureland in the Magic Kingdom is the all-time worst for disorienting visitors. Children and adults alike have walked in from the Adventureland side and walked out on the Frontierland side (and vice versa). Adults realize quickly that something is wrong. Young children, however, sometimes fail to recognize the problem. Designate a meeting spot more distinctive than a bench, and be thorough in your instructions: "I'll meet you by this flagpole. If you get out first, stay right here." Have your child repeat the directions back to you.

5. Parades   There are many parades and shows at which the audience stands. Children tend to jockey for a better view. By moving a little this way and that, the child quickly puts distance between you before either of you notices.

6. Mass Movements   Be on guard when huge crowds disperse after fireworks or a parade, or at park closing. With 20,000 to 40,000 people at once in an area, it's very easy to get separated from a child or others in your party. Use extra caution after the evening parade and fireworks in the Magic Kingdom, *Fantasmic!* at the Disney-MGM Studios, or *IllumiNations* at Epcot. Families should have specific plans for where to meet if they get separated.

7. Character Greetings   Activity and confusion are common when the Disney characters appear, and children can slip out of sight. See "Then Some Confusion Happened" (page 132).

8. Getting Lost at the Animal Kingdom   It's especially easy to lose a child at the Animal Kingdom, particularly in the Oasis entryway, on the Maharaja Jungle Trek, and on the Gorilla Falls Exploration Trail. Mom and dad will stop to observe an animal. Junior stays close for a minute or so, and then, losing patience, wanders to the other side of the exhibit or to a different exhibit.

Part Six

The Magic Kingdom

At the Magic Kingdom, stroller and wheelchair rentals are to the right of the train station, and lockers are on the station's ground floor. On your left as you enter Main Street is City Hall, the center for information, lost and found, guided tours, and entertainment schedules.

If you don't already have a handout guidemap of the park, get one at City Hall. The guidemap lists all attractions, shops, and eating places; provides helpful information about first aid, baby care, and assistance for the disabled; and gives tips for good photos. It also lists times for the day's special events, live entertainment, Disney character parades, concerts, and other activities. Also available at City Hall is the *Disney Character Greeting Location Guide,* telling when and where to find Disney characters.

Main Street ends at a central hub from which branch the entrances to five other sections of the Magic Kingdom: Adventureland, Frontierland, Liberty Square, Fantasyland, and Tomorrowland. Mickey's Toontown Fair doesn't connect to the central hub—it is wedged like a dimple between the cheeks of Fantasyland and Tomorrowland.

In this and the following three chapters we rate the individual attractions at each of the four major Disney theme parks. The author's rating as well as ratings according to age group are on a scale of zero to five stars—the more stars, the better the attraction. The author's rating is from the perspective of an adult. The author, for example, might rate a ride such as Dumbo much lower than the age group for which the ride is intended, in this case, children. His rating, therefore, will more closely approximate

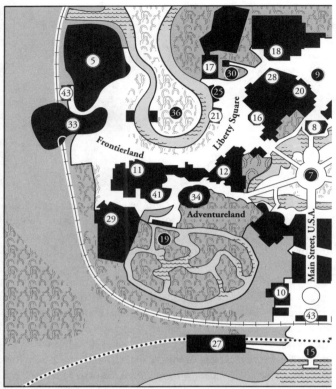

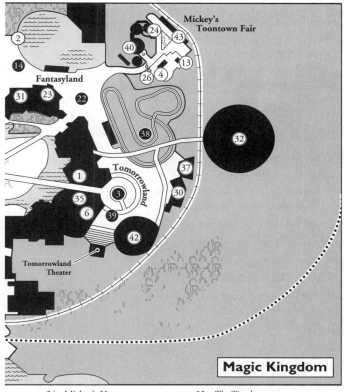

Mickey's
Toontown Fair

Fantasyland

Tomorrowland

Tomorrowland
Theater

Magic Kingdom

24. Mickey's House
25. Mike Fink Keelboats
26. Minnie's House
27. Monorail Station
28. Peter Pan's Flight
29. Pirates of the Caribbean
30. Skyway
31. Snow White's Adventures
32. Space Mountain
33. Splash Mountain
34. Swiss Family Treehouse

35. *The Timekeeper*
36. Tom Sawyer Island
37. Tomorrowland Arcade
38. Tomorrowland Speedway
39. Tomorrowland Transit Authority
40. Toontown Hall of Fame
41. *Tropical Serenade
    (Enchanted Tiki Birds)*
42. Walt Disney's *Carousel of Progress*
43. WDW Railroad Station

how another adult will experience the attraction than how your children will like it. The bottleneck rating ranges from one to ten; the higher the rating, the more congested the attraction. In general, try to experience attractions with a high bottleneck rating early in the morning (that is, between 8 and 10 a.m.) before the park gets crowded or late in the day when the crowd has diminished.

Main Street, U.S.A.

Walt Disney World Railroad

What It Is: Scenic railroad ride around perimeter of the Magic Kingdom, and transportation to Frontierland and Mickey's Toontown Fair

Scope & Scale: Minor attraction

Fright Potential: Not frightening in any respect

Bottleneck Rating: 6

When to Go: Anytime

Author's Rating: Plenty to see; ★★★

Appeal by Age Group:

Pre-school	Grade School	Teens	Young Adults	Senior Over 30	Citizens
★★★★	★★★	★★	★★½	★★★	★★★

Duration of Ride: About 19 minutes for a complete circuit

Average Wait in Line per 100 People ahead of You: 8 minutes

Adventureland

Adventureland is the first land to the left of Main Street. It combines an African safari theme with an old New Orleans/Caribbean atmosphere.

Swiss Family Treehouse

What It Is: Outdoor walk-through treehouse

Scope & Scale: Minor attraction

Fright Potential: Not frightening in any respect

Bottleneck Rating: 6

When to Go: Before 11:30 a.m. and after 5 p.m.

Special Comments: Requires climbing a lot of stairs

Author's Rating: A visual delight; ★★★

Appeal by Age Group:

Pre-school	Grade School	Teens	Young Adults	Over 30	Senior Citizens
★★★	★★★½	★★★	★★★	★★★	★★★

Duration of Tour: 10–15 minutes

Average Wait in Line per 100 People ahead of You: 7 minutes

Jungle Cruise

What It Is: Outdoor safari-themed boat ride adventure

Scope & Scale: Major attraction

Fright Potential: Moderately intense, some macabre sights; a good test attraction for little ones

Bottleneck Rating: 10

When to Go: Before 10 a.m. or two hours before closing

Author's Rating: A long-enduring Disney masterpiece; ★★★

Appeal by Age Group:

Pre-school	Grade School	Teens	Young Adults	Over 30	Senior Citizens
★★★½	★★★½	★★½	★★★	★★★	★★★

Duration of Ride: 8–9 minutes

Average Wait in Line per 100 People ahead of You: 3½ minutes

Pirates of the Caribbean

What It Is: Indoor pirate-themed adventure boat ride

Scope & Scale: Headliner

Fright Potential: Slightly intimidating queuing area; intense boat ride with gruesome (though humorously presented) sights and a short, unexpected slide down a flume

Bottleneck Rating: 7

When to Go: Before noon or after 5 p.m.

Author's Rating: Disney Audio-Animatronics at its best; not to be missed; ★★★★★

Appeal by Age Group:

Pre-school	Grade School	Teens	Young Adults	Over 30	Senior Citizens
★★★	★★★★★	★★★★	★★★★	★★★★½	★★★★½

Duration of Ride: About 7½ minutes

Average Wait in Line per 100 People ahead of You: 1½ minutes

Tropical Serenade (Enchanted Tiki Birds)

What It Is: Audio-Animatronic Pacific island musical theater show

Scope & Scale: Minor attraction

Fright Potential: A thunderstorm momentarily surprises very young children

Bottleneck Rating: 4

When to Go: Before 11 a.m. and after 3:30 p.m.

Author's Rating: Revised and upgraded in 1998; ★★★½

Appeal by Age Group:

Pre-school	Grade School	Teens	Young Adults	Over 30	Senior Citizens
★★★★	★★★½	★★★	★★★	★★★	★★★½

Duration of Presentation: 15½ minutes

Preshow Entertainment: Talking birds

Probable Waiting Time: 15 minutes

Frontierland

Frontierland adjoins Adventureland as you move clockwise around the Magic Kingdom. The focus is on the Old West, with stockade-type structures and pioneer trappings.

Splash Mountain

What It Is: Indoor/outdoor water-flume adventure ride

Scope & Scale: Super headliner

Fright Potential: Visually intimidating from outside, with moderately intense visual effects. The ride, culminating in a 52-foot plunge down a steep chute, is somewhat hair-raising for all ages. Switching off option provided

Bottleneck Rating: 10

When to Go: As soon as the park opens, during afternoon or evening parades, or just before closing

Special Comments: Children must be 40" tall to ride; those younger than age 7 must ride with an adult. Switching off option provided

Author's Rating: A wet winner; not to be missed; ★★★★★

Appeal by Age Group:

Pre-school	Grade School	Teens	Young Adults	Over 30	Senior Citizens
†	★★★★★	★★★★★	★★★★★	★★★★★	★★★½

† Many preschoolers are too short to meet the height requirement, and others are visually intimidated when they see the ride from the waiting line. Among preschoolers who actually ride, most give the attraction high marks (3–5 stars)

Duration of Ride: About 10 minutes

Average Wait in Line per 100 People ahead of You: 3½ minutes

Big Thunder Mountain Railroad

What It Is: Tame, Western mining–themed roller coaster

Scope & Scale: Headliner

Fright Potential: Visually intimidating from outside, with moderately intense visual effects; the roller coaster is wild enough to frighten many adults, particularly seniors

Bottleneck Rating: 9

When to Go: Before 10 a.m. or in the hour before closing

Special Comments: Children must be 40" tall to ride. Those younger than age 7 must ride with an adult. Switching off option provided

Author's Rating: Great effects; relatively tame ride; not to be missed; ★★★★

Appeal by Age Group:

Pre-school	Grade School	Teens	Young Adults	Over 30	Senior Citizens
★★★	★★★★	★★★★	★★★★	★★★★	★★★

Duration of Ride: Almost 3½ minutes

Average Wait in Line per 100 People ahead of You: 2½ minutes

Country Bear Jamboree

What It Is: Audio-Animatronic country hoedown theater show

Scope & Scale: Major attraction

Fright Potential: Not frightening in any respect

Bottleneck Rating: 8

When to Go: Before 11:30 a.m., before a parade, or during the two hours before closing

Special Comments: Shows change at Christmas and during summer

Author's Rating: A Disney classic; ★★★

Appeal by Age Group:

Pre-school	Grade School	Teens	Young Adults	Over 30	Senior Citizens
★★★½	★★★	★★½	★★★	★★★	★★★

Duration of Presentation: 15 minutes

Preshow Entertainment: None

Probable Waiting Time: This attraction is very popular but has a comparatively small capacity. Waiting time between noon and 5:30 p.m. on a busy day will average 30–50 minutes

Tom Sawyer Island and Fort Sam Clemens

What It Is: Outdoor walk-through exhibit/rustic playground

Scope & Scale: Minor attraction

Fright Potential: Some very young children are intimidated by dark, walk-through tunnels that can be easily avoided

Bottleneck Rating: 4

When to Go: Midmorning through late afternoon

Special Comments: Closes at dusk

Author's Rating: The place for rambunctious kids; ★★★

Appeal by Age Group:

Pre-school	Grade School	Teens	Young Adults	Over 30	Senior Citizens
★★★★★	★★★★★	★★	★★	★★	★★

The Diamond Horseshoe Saloon Revue

What It Is: Live western song-and-dance show

Scope & Scale: Minor attraction

Fright Potential: Occasional loud noises startle infants and toddlers

Bottleneck Rating: 6

When to Go: Check the daily entertainment schedule

Special Comments: No Disney characters appear in this show.
Food served, so catch the show over lunch or a snack break

Author's Rating: Fast-paced and funny; ★★★

Appeal by Age Group:

Pre-school	Grade School	Teens	Young Adults	Over 30	Senior Citizens
★★	★★★	★★	★★★½	★★★½	★★★½

Duration of Show: About 40 minutes

Average Wait in Line per 100 People ahead of You: No wait

Liberty Square

Liberty Square re-creates Colonial America at the time of the
American Revolution. The architecture is Federal or Colonial. A
real, 130-year-old live oak (dubbed the "Liberty Tree") lends dig-
nity and grace to the setting.

The Hall of Presidents

What It Is: Audio-Animatronic historical theater presentation

Scope & Scale: Major attraction

Fright Potential: Not frightening in any respect

Bottleneck Rating: 4

When to Go: Anytime

Author's Rating: Impressive and moving; ★★★

Appeal by Age Group:

Pre-school	Grade School	Teens	Young Adults	Over 30	Senior Citizens
★	★★½	★★★	★★★½	★★★★	★★★★

Duration of Presentation: Almost 23 minutes

Preshow Entertainment: None

Probable Waiting Time: Lines for this attraction appear awesome
but are usually swallowed up as the theater exchanges audi-
ences. Your wait will probably be the remaining time of the

show that's in progress when you arrive. Even during the busiest times of day, waits rarely exceed 40 minutes.

Liberty Belle Riverboat

What It Is: Outdoor scenic boat ride

Scope & Scale: Major attraction

Fright Potential: Not frightening in any respect

Bottleneck Rating: 4

When to Go: Anytime

Author's Rating: Slow, relaxing, and scenic; ★★★

Appeal by Age Group:

Pre-school	Grade School	Teens	Young Adults	Over 30	Senior Citizens
★★★½	★★★	★★½	★★★	★★★	★★★

Duration of Ride: About 16 minutes

Average Wait to Board: 10–14 minutes

The Haunted Mansion

What It Is: Haunted-house track ride

Scope & Scale: Major attraction

Fright Potential: Name raises anxiety, as do sounds and sights of waiting area. Intense attraction with humorously presented macabre sights. The ride itself is gentle

Bottleneck Rating: 8

When to Go: Before 11:30 a.m. or after 8 p.m.

Special Comments: Frightens some very young children

Author's Rating: Not to be missed; ★★★★

Appeal by Age Group:

Pre-school	Grade School	Teens	Young Adults	Over 30	Senior Citizens
(Varies)	★★★★★	★★★★	★★★★	★★★★	★★★★

Duration of Ride: 7-minute ride plus a 1½-minute preshow

Average Wait in Line per 100 People ahead of You: 2½ minutes

Mike Fink Keelboats

What It Is: Outdoor scenic boat ride

Scope & Scale: Minor attraction

Fright Potential: Not frightening in any respect

Bottleneck Rating: 9

When to Go: Before 11:30 a.m. or after 5 p.m.

Special Comments: Don't ride if the lines are long; closes at dusk

Author's Rating: ★★

Appeal by Age Group:

Pre-school	Grade School	Teens	Young Adults	Over 30	Senior Citizens
★★★	★★★	★★½	★★½	★★½	★★½

Duration of Ride: 9½ minutes

Average Wait in Line per 100 People ahead of You: 15 minutes

Fantasyland

Fantasyland is the heart of the Magic Kingdom, a truly enchanting place spread gracefully like a miniature Alpine village beneath the lofty towers of the Cinderella Castle.

It's a Small World

What It Is: World brotherhood–themed indoor boat ride

Scope & Scale: Major attraction

When to Go: Anytime

Fright Potential: Not frightening in any respect

Bottleneck Rating: 6

Author's Rating: Exponentially "cute"; ★★★

Appeal by Age Group:

Pre-school	Grade School	Teens	Young Adults	Over 30	Senior Citizens
★★★½	★★★	★★½	★★½	★★½	★★★

Duration of Ride: Approximately 11 minutes

Average Wait in Line per 100 People ahead of You: 11 minutes

Skyway to Tomorrowland

What It Is: Scenic transportation to Tomorrowland

Scope & Scale: Minor attraction

Fright Potential: Not frightening in any respect

Bottleneck Rating: 9

When to Go: Before noon or during special events

Special Comments: If there's a line, it probably will be quicker to walk

Author's Rating: Nice view; ★★★

Appeal by Age Group:

Pre-school	Grade School	Teens	Young Adults	Over 30	Senior Citizens
★★★★	★★★★	★★★	★★★	★★★	★★★

Duration of Ride: About 5 minutes one way

Average Wait in Line per 100 People ahead of You: 10 minutes

Peter Pan's Flight

What It Is: Indoor track ride

Scope & Scale: Minor attraction

Fright Potential: Not frightening in any respect.

Bottleneck Rating: 8

When to Go: Before 10 a.m. or after 6 p.m.

Author's Rating: Happy, mellow, and well done; ★★★★

Appeal by Age Group:

Pre-school	Grade School	Teens	Young Adults	Over 30	Senior Citizens
★★★½	★★★½	★★★½	★★★½	★★★½	★★★½

Duration of Ride: A little over 3 minutes

Average Wait in Line per 100 People ahead of You: 5½ minutes

Legend of the Lion King

What It Is: Live mixed-media and puppet theater show

Scope & Scale: Major attraction

Fright Potential: Sudden loud noise and music startles very young children

Bottleneck Rating: 8

When to Go: Before 11 a.m. and during parades

Author's Rating: Uplifting and fun; ★★★

Appeal by Age Group:

Preschool	Grade School	Teens	Young Adults	Over 30	Senior Citizens
★★★	★★★½	★★★	★★★	★★★	★★★

Duration of Presentation: About 16 minutes

Preshow Entertainment: 7-minute preshow

Probable Waiting Time: 12 minutes (before 10:30 a.m.)

Cinderella's Golden Carrousel

What It Is: Merry-go-round

Scope & Scale: Minor attraction

Fright Potential: Not frightening in any respect

Bottleneck Rating: 9

When to Go: Before 11 a.m. or after 8 p.m.

Special Comments: Adults enjoy the beauty and nostalgia of this ride

Author's Rating: A beautiful children's ride; ★★★

Appeal by Age Group:

Preschool	Grade School	Teens	Young Adults	Over 30	Senior Citizens
★★★★	★★½	N/A	N/A	N/A	N/A

Duration of Ride: About 2 minutes

Average Wait in Line per 100 People ahead of You: 5 minutes

The Many Adventures of Winnie the Pooh

What It Is: Indoor track ride

Scope & Scale: Minor attraction

Fright Potential: Not frightening in any respect

Bottleneck Rating: 8

When to Go: Before 10 a.m. or in the 2 hours before closing

Author's Rating: New home for a favorite character; ★★★½

Appeal by Age Group:

Pre-school	Grade School	Teens	Young Adults	Over 30	Senior Citizens
★★★★	★★★★	★★★	★★★	★★★	★★★

Duration of Ride: About 4 minutes

Average Wait in Line per 100 People ahead of You: 5 minutes

Snow White's Adventures

What It Is: Indoor track ride

Scope & Scale: Minor attraction

Fright Potential: Moderately intense spook-house-genre attraction with some grim characters. Terrifies many preschoolers

Bottleneck Rating: 8

When to Go: Before 11 a.m. and after 6 p.m.

Special Comments: Terrifying to many young children

Author's Rating: Worth seeing if the wait isn't long; ★★½

Appeal by Age Group:

Pre-school	Grade School	Teens	Young Adults	Over 30	Senior Citizens
★	★★½	★★	★★½	★★½	★★½

Duration of Ride: Almost 2½ minutes

Average Wait in Line per 100 People ahead of You: 6½ minutes

Ariel's Grotto

What It Is: Interactive fountain and character greeting area

Scope & Scale: Minor attraction

Fright Potential: Not frightening in any respect

Bottleneck Rating: 9

When to Go: Before 10 a.m. and after 9 p.m.

Author's Rating: One of the most elaborate of the character-greeting venues; ★★★

Appeal by Age Group:

Pre-school	Grade School	Teens	Young Adults	Over 30	Senior Citizens
★★★★★	★★★½	★	★	★	★

Average Wait in Line per 100 People ahead of You: 30 minutes

Dumbo the Flying Elephant

What It Is: Disneyfied midway ride

Scope & Scale: Minor attraction

Fright Potential: A tame midway ride; a great favorite of most young children

Bottleneck Rating: 10

When to Go: Before 10 a.m. and after 9 p.m.

Author's Rating: An attractive children's ride; ★★★

Appeal by Age Group:

Pre-school	Grade School	Teens	Young Adults	Over 30	Senior Citizens
★★★★★	★★★★	★½	★½	★½	★½

Duration of Ride: 1½ minutes

Average Wait in Line per 100 People ahead of You: 20 minutes

Mad Tea Party

What It Is: Midway-type spinning ride

Scope & Scale: Minor attraction

Fright Potential: Midway-type ride can induce motion sickness in all ages

Bottleneck Rating: 9

When to Go: Before 11 a.m. and after 5 p.m.

Special Comments: You can make the teacups spin faster by turning the wheel in the center of the cup

Author's Rating: Fun, but not worth the wait; ★★

Appeal by Age Group:

Pre-school	Grade School	Teens	Young Adults	Over 30	Senior Citizens
★★★★	★★★★	★★★★	★★★	★★	★★

Duration of Ride: 1½ minutes

Average Wait in Line per 100 People ahead of You: 7½ minutes

Assumes: Normal staffing

Mickey's Toontown Fair

Mickey's Toontown Fair is the first new "land" to be added to the Magic Kingdom since its opening and the only one that doesn't connect to the central hub. Attractions include an opportunity to meet Mickey Mouse, Mickey's house, Minnie Mouse's house, and a child-size roller coaster.

Mickey's Country House & Judge's Tent

What It Is: Walk-through tour of Mickey's house and meeting with Mickey

Scope & Scale: Minor attraction

Fright Potential: Not frightening in any respect

Bottleneck Rating: 9

When to Go: Before 11:30 a.m. and after 4:30 p.m.

Author's Rating: Well done; ★★★

Appeal by Age Group:

Pre-school	Grade School	Teens	Young Adults	Over 30	Senior Citizens
★★★½	★★★	★★½	★★½	★★½	★★½

Duration of Tour: 15–30 minutes (depending on the crowd)

Average Wait in Line per 100 People ahead of You: 20 minutes

Minnie's Country House

What It Is: Walk-through exhibit

Scope & Scale: Minor attraction

Fright Potential: Not frightening in any respect

Bottleneck Rating: 9

When to Go: Before 11:30 a.m. and after 4:30 p.m.

Author's Rating: Great detail; ★★

Appeal by Age Group:

Pre-school	Grade School	Teens	Young Adults	Over 30	Senior Citizens
★★★	★★★	★★½	★★½	★★½	★★½

Duration of Tour: About 10 minutes

Average Wait in Line per 100 People ahead of You: 12 minutes

Toontown Hall of Fame

What It Is: Character-greeting venue

Scope & Scale: Minor attraction

Fright Potential: Not frightening in any respect

Bottleneck Rating: 10

When to Go: Before 10:30 a.m. and after 5:30 p.m.

Author's Rating: You want characters? We got 'em! ★★

Appeal by Age Group:

Pre-school	Grade School	Teens	Young Adults	Over 30	Senior Citizens
★★★★	★★★★	★★	★★	★★	★★

Duration of Greeting: About 7–10 minutes

Average Wait in Line per 100 People ahead of You: 35 minutes

The Barnstormer at Goofy's Wiseacres Farm

What It Is: Small roller coaster

Scope & Scale: Minor attraction

Fright Potential: A children's coaster; frightens some preschoolers

Bottleneck Rating: 9

When to Go: Before 10:30 a.m., during parades and in the evening, and just before the park closes

Author's Rating: Great for little ones as an introduction to thrill rides; ★★

Appeal by Age Group:

Pre-school	Grade School	Teens	Young Adults	Over 30	Senior Citizens
★★★★	★★★	★½	★★½	★★½	★★

Duration of Ride: About 53 seconds

Average Wait in Line per 100 People ahead of You: 7 minutes

Donald's Boat

What It Is: Interactive fountain and playground

Scope & Scale: Diversion

Fright Potential: Not frightening in any respect

Bottleneck Rating: 3

When to Go: Anytime
Special Comments: Children can get wet
Author's Rating: Spontaneous—yeah! ★★½
Appeal by Age Group:

Pre-school	Grade School	Teens	Young Adults	Over 30	Senior Citizens
★★★★	★★½	★	★½	★½	★½

Tomorrowland

Tomorrowland is a mix of rides and experiences relating to the technological development of humankind and what life will be like in the future. An exhaustive renovation of Tomorrowland was completed in 1995.

Space Mountain

What It Is: Roller coaster in the dark

Scope & Scale: Super headliner

Fright Potential: Very intense roller coaster in the dark; the Magic Kingdom's wildest ride and a scary roller coaster by any standard. Switching off provided

Bottleneck Rating: 10

When to Go: First thing when the park opens, between 6 and 7 p.m., or during the hour before closing

Special Comments: Great fun and action; much wilder than Big Thunder Mountain Railroad. Children must be 44" tall to ride, and if younger than age 7, must be accompanied by an adult

Author's Rating: A great roller coaster with excellent special effects; not to be missed; ★★★★

Appeal by Age Group:

Pre-school	Grade School	Teens	Young Adults	Over 30	Senior Citizens
†	★★★★★	★★★★★	★★★★½	★★★★	†

† Some preschoolers loved Space Mountain; others were frightened. The sample size of senior citizens who experienced this ride was too small to develop an accurate rating

Duration of Ride: Almost 3 minutes

Average Wait in Line per 100 People ahead of You: 3 minutes

Tomorrowland Speedway

What It Is: Drive-'em-yourself miniature cars

Scope & Scale: Major attraction

Fright Potential: Not frightening in any respect

Bottleneck Rating: 9

When to Go: Before 11 a.m. and after 5 p.m.

Special Comments: Must be 52" tall to drive, but kids can steer while parent works the pedals

Author's Rating: Boring for adults (★); great for preschoolers

Appeal by Age Group:

Pre-school	Grade School	Teens	Young Adults	Over 30	Senior Citizens
★★★★	★★★	★	½	½	½

Duration of Ride: About 4¼ minutes

Average Wait in Line per 100 People ahead of You: 4½ minutes

Skyway to Fantasyland

What It Is: Scenic overhead transportation to Fantasyland

Scope & Scale: Minor attraction

Fright Potential: Not frightening in any respect

Bottleneck Rating: 9

When to Go: Before noon and during special events

Special Comments: If there's a line, it's probably quicker to walk

Author's Rating: Nice view; ★★★

Appeal by Age Group:

Pre-school	Grade School	Teens	Young Adults	Over 30	Senior Citizens
★★★★	★★★★	★★★	★★★	★★★	★★★

Duration of Ride: Approximately 5 minutes one-way

Average Wait in Line per 100 People ahead of You: 10 minutes

Astro Orbiter

What It Is: Buck Rogers–style rockets revolving around a central axis

Scope & Scale: Minor attraction

Fright Potential: Visually intimidating from the waiting area. The ride is relatively tame

Bottleneck Rating: 10

When to Go: Before 11 a.m. or after 5 p.m.

Author's Rating: Not worth the wait; ★★

Appeal by Age Group:

Pre-school	Grade School	Teens	Young Adults	Over 30	Senior Citizens
★★★★	★★★	★★½	★★½	★★	★

Duration of Ride: 1½ minutes

Average Wait in Line per 100 People ahead of You: 13½ minutes

Tomorrowland Transit Authority

What It Is: Scenic tour of Tomorrowland

Scope & Scale: Minor attraction

Fright Potential: Not frightening in any respect

Bottleneck Rating: 3

When to Go: During hot, crowded times of day (11:30 a.m.–4:30 p.m.)

Special Comments: A good way to check out the crowd at Space Mountain

Author's Rating: Scenic, relaxing, informative; ★★★

Appeal by Age Group:

Pre-school	Grade School	Teens	Young Adults	Over 30	Senior Citizens
★★★½	★★★	★★½	★★½	★★½	★★★

Duration of Ride: 10 minutes

Average Wait in Line per 100 People ahead of You: 1½ minutes

Walt Disney's Carousel of Progress

What It Is: Audio-Animatronic theater production

Scope & Scale: Major attraction

Fright Potential: Not frightening in any respect

Bottleneck Rating: 4

When to Go: Anytime

Author's Rating: Nostalgic, warm, and happy; ★★★

Appeal by Age Group:

Pre-school	Grade School	Teens	Young Adults	Over 30	Senior Citizens
★★	★★½	★★½	★★★	★★★	★★★½

Duration of Presentation: 18 minutes

Preshow Entertainment: Documentary on the attraction's long history

Probable Waiting Time: Less than 10 minutes

Buzz Lightyear's Space Ranger Spin

What It Is: Whimsical space travel–themed indoor ride

Scope & Scale: Minor attraction

Fright Potential: Dark ride with cartoonlike aliens may frighten some preschoolers

Bottleneck Rating: 5

When to Go: Anytime

Author's Rating: Lighthearted and high-tech; ★★★

Appeal by Age Group:

Pre-school	Grade School	Teens	Young Adults	Over 30	Senior Citizens
★★★★	★★★★	★★★	★★★	★★★	★★★

Duration of Ride: About 4½ minutes

Average Wait in Line per 100 People ahead of You: 3 minutes

The Timekeeper

What It Is: Time-travel movie adventure

Scope & Scale: Major attraction

Fright Potential: Intense, loud; audience must stand

Bottleneck Rating: 5

When to Go: Anytime

Special Comments: Audience must stand throughout presentation

Author's Rating: Outstanding; not to be missed; ★★★★

Appeal by Age Group:

Pre-school	Grade School	Teens	Young Adults	Over 30	Senior Citizens
★★	★★★½	★★★½	★★★½	★★★★	★★★★

Duration of Presentation: About 20 minutes

Preshow Entertainment: Robots, lasers, and movies

Probable Waiting Time: 8–15 minutes

Alien Encounter

What It Is: Theater-in-the-round sci-fi horror show

Scope & Scale: Headliner

Fright Potential: Extremely intense. Capable of frightening all ages. Not for young children. Switching off provided

Bottleneck Rating: 9

When to Go: Before 10 a.m. or after 6 p.m.; try during parades

Special Comments: Frightens children of all ages

Author's Rating: ★★★

Appeal by Age Group:

Pre-school	Grade School	Teens	Young Adults	Over 30	Senior Citizens
N/A	★★★★	★★★★	★★★★	★★★★	★★★

Duration of Presentation: About 12 minutes

Preshow Entertainment: About 6 minutes

Probable Waiting Time: 12–40 minutes

Parades

An afternoon parade always takes place. When the park is open past 8 p.m., there are also evening parades and fireworks. The best viewing spots for the parades are in Liberty Square, while the best viewing spot for the fireworks is the veranda of the Plaza pavilion restaurant in Tomorrowland. For parade and fireworks times, consult the daily entertainment schedule on the back of the park handout map.

Part Seven

Epcot

Education, inspiration, and corporate imagery are the focus at Epcot, the most adult of the Walt Disney World theme parks. What it gains in taking a futuristic, visionary, and technological look at the world, it loses, just a bit, in warmth, happiness, and charm. Some people find the attempts at education to be superficial; others want more entertainment and less education. Most visitors, however, are in between, finding plenty of entertainment and education.

Epcot's theme areas are distinctly different. Future World combines Disney creativity and major corporations' technological resources to examine where humankind has come from and where we're going. World Showcase features landmarks, cuisine, and culture of almost a dozen nations and is meant to be a sort of permanent World's Fair.

Most Epcot services are concentrated in Future World's Entrance Plaza, near the main gate. The Baby Center is on the World Showcase side of the Odyssey Center, between the World Showcase and Future World.

Future World

Spaceship Earth

What It Is: Educational dark ride through past, present, and future

Scope & Scale: Headliner

Fright Potential: Dark and imposing presentation intimidates a few preschoolers

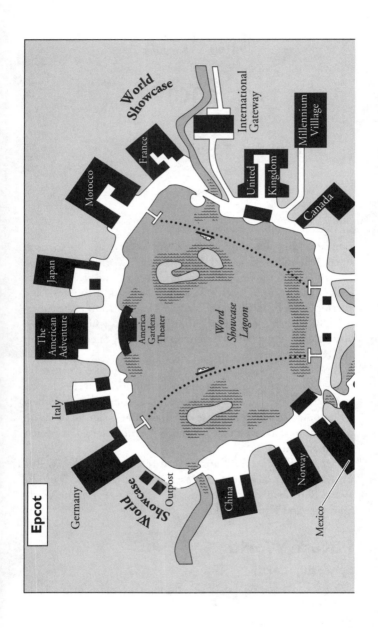

Epcot

World Showcase

International Gateway

Millennium Village

United Kingdom

Canada

France

Morocco

Japan

The American Adventure

America Gardens Theater

Word Showcase Lagoon

Italy

Germany

World Showcase

Outpost

China

Norway

Mexico

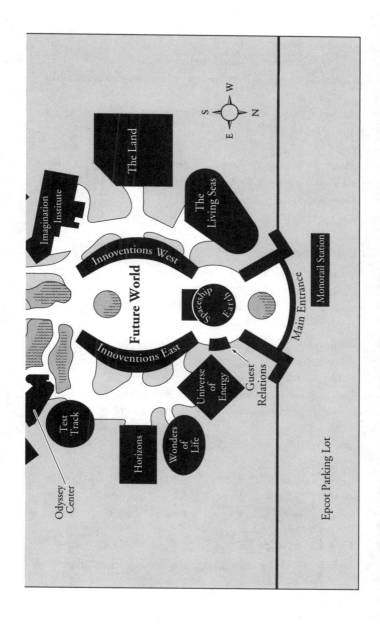

Bottleneck Rating: 7

When to Go: Before 10 a.m. or after 4 p.m.

Special Comments: If lines are long when you arrive, try again after 4 p.m.

Author's Rating: One of Epcot's best; not to be missed; ★★★★

Appeal by Age Group:

Pre-school	Grade School	Teens	Young Adults	Over 30	Senior Citizens
★★★	★★★★	★★★½	★★★★	★★★★	★★★★

Duration of Ride: About 16 minutes

Average Wait in Line per 100 People ahead of You: 3 minutes

INNOVENTIONS

What It Is: Static and hands-on exhibits relating to products and technologies of the near future

Scope & Scale: Major diversion

Fright Potential: Not frightening in any respect

Bottleneck Rating: 8

When to Go: On your second day at Epcot or after you have seen all major attractions

Special Comments: Most exhibits demand time and participation to be rewarding; not much gained here by a quick walk-through

Author's Rating: Vastly improved; ★★★½

Appeal by Age Group:

Pre-school	Grade School	Teens	Young Adults	Over 30	Senior Citizens
★½	★★★½	★★★★	★★★½	★★★	★★★

THE LIVING SEAS

What It Is: Ride beneath a huge saltwater aquarium, plus exhibits on oceanography, ocean ecology, and sea life

Scope & Scale: Major attraction

Fright Potential: Not frightening in any respect

Bottleneck Rating: 7

When to Go: Before 10 a.m. or after 3 p.m.

Special Comments: The ride is only a small component of this attraction

Author's Rating: An excellent marine exhibit; ★★★½

Appeal by Age Group:

Pre-school	Grade School	Teens	Young Adults	Over 30	Senior Citizens
★★★	★★★	★★★	★★★★	★★★★	★★★★

Duration of Ride: 3 minutes

Average Wait in Line per 100 People ahead of You: 3½ minutes

THE LAND PAVILION

The Land is a huge pavilion containing three attractions and several restaurants. It was extensively renovated in 1994, and its three attractions were updated and improved. The original emphasis was on farming, but it now focuses on environmental concerns.

Living with the Land

What It Is: Indoor boat-ride adventure through the past, present, and future of U.S. farming and agriculture

Scope & Scale: Major attraction

Fright Potential: Not frightening in any respect

Bottleneck Rating: 9

When to Go: Before 10:30 a.m. or after 7:30 p.m.

Special Comments: Take the ride early in the morning, but save other Land attractions for later in the day. It's on the pavilion's lower level

Author's Rating: Interesting and fun; not to be missed; ★★★★

Appeal by Age Group:

Pre-school	Grade School	Teens	Young Adults	Over 30	Senior Citizens
★★½	★★★	★★★½	★★★★	★★★★	★★★★

Duration of Ride: About 12 minutes

Average Wait in Line per 100 People ahead of You: 3 minutes

Food Rocks

What It Is: Audio-Animatronic theater show about food and nutrition

Scope & Scale: Minor attraction

Fright Potential: Not frightening in any respect, but loud

Bottleneck Rating: 5

When to Go: Before 11 a.m. or after 2 p.m.

Special Comments: On the lower level of The Land pavilion

Author's Rating: Sugar-coated nutrition lesson; ★★★

Appeal by Age Group:

Pre-school	Grade School	Teens	Young Adults	Over 30	Senior Citizens
★★★	★★★	★★½	★★★	★★★	★★★

Duration of Presentation: About 13 minutes

Preshow Entertainment: None

Probable Waiting Time: Less than 10 minutes

Circle of Life Theater

What It Is: Film exploring humankind's relationship with the environment

Scope & Scale: Minor attraction

Fright Potential: Not frightening in any respect

Bottleneck Rating: 5

When to Go: Before 11 a.m. and after 2 p.m.

Author's Rating: Highly interesting and enlightening; ★★★½

Appeal by Age Group:

Pre-school	Grade School	Teens	Young Adults	Over 30	Senior Citizens
★★½	★★★	★★½	★★★	★★★	★★★

Duration of Presentation: About 12½ minutes

Preshow Entertainment: None

Probable Waiting Time: 10–15 minutes

IMAGINATION INSTITUTE PAVILION

Multiattraction pavilion on the west side of Innoventions West and down the walk from The Land. Outside is an "upside-down waterfall" and one of our favorite Future World landmarks, the "jumping water," a fountain that hops over the heads of unsuspecting passersby. The building houses three attractions.

Journey into Your Imagination Ride

What It Is: Dark fantasy-adventure ride

Scope & Scale: Major attraction

Fright Potential:

When to Go: Before 10:30 a.m. or after 6 p.m.

Author's Rating: Not open at press time

Appeal by Age Group:

Pre-school	Grade School	Teens	Young Adults	Over 30	Senior Citizens
Not open at press time					

Duration of Ride: About 13 minutes

Average Wait in Line per 100 People ahead of You: 3 minutes

Honey, I Shrunk the Audience

What It Is: 3D film with special effects

Scope & Scale: Headliner

Fright Potential: Extremely intense visual effects and loudness frighten many young children

Bottleneck Rating: 10

When to Go: Before 10 a.m. or just before Future World closes

Special Comments: Adults should not be put off by the sci-fi theme. The loud, intense show with tactile effects frightens some young children

Author's Rating: An absolute hoot! Not to be missed; ★★★★½

Appeal by Age Group:

Pre-school	Grade School	Teens	Young Adults	Over 30	Senior Citizens
★★★	★★★★½	★★★★½	★★★★½	★★★★½	★★★★

Duration of Presentation: About 17 minutes
Preshow Entertainment: 8 minutes
Probable Waiting Time: 12 minutes (at suggested times)

Test Track

What It Is: Automobile test-track simulator ride
Scope & Scale: Super headliner
Fright Potential: Intense thrill ride may frighten guests of any
    age. Switching off provided.
Bottleneck Rating: 10
When to Go: Before 9:15 a.m. and just before closing
Author's Rating: Not to be missed; ★★★★
Appeal by Age Group:

Pre-school	Grade School	Teens	Young Adults	Over 30	Senior Citizens
★★★	★★★★	★★★★	★★★★	★★★★	★★★★

Duration of Ride: About 4 minutes
Average Wait in Line per 100 People ahead of You: 4½ minutes

WONDERS OF LIFE PAVILION

This multifaceted pavilion deals with the human body, health,
and medicine. Housed in a 100,000-square-foot, gold-domed
structure, Wonders of Life focuses on the capabilities of the
human body and the importance of keeping fit.

Body Wars

What It Is: Flight-simulator ride through the human body
Scope & Scale: Headliner
Fright Potential: Very intense, with frightening visual effects.
    Ride causes motion sickness in susceptible riders of all ages.
    Switching off provided
Bottleneck Rating: 9
When to Go: Before 10 a.m. or after 6 p.m.
Special Comments: Not recommended for pregnant women or
    people prone to motion sickness
Author's Rating: Anatomy made fun; not to be missed; ★★★★

Appeal by Age Group:

Pre-school	Grade School	Teens	Young Adults	Over 30	Senior Citizens
★★★	★★★★	★★★★	★★★★	★★★★½	★★½

Duration of Ride: 5 minutes

Average Wait in Line per 100 People ahead of You: 4 minutes

Cranium Command

What It Is: Audio-Animatronic theater show about the brain

Scope & Scale: Major attraction

Fright Potential: Not frightening in any respect

Bottleneck Rating: 5

When to Go: Before 11 a.m. or after 3 p.m.

Author's Rating: Funny, outrageous, and educational; not to be missed; ★★★★½

Appeal by Age Group:

Pre-school	Grade School	Teens	Young Adults	Over 30	Senior Citizens
★★	★★★★	★★★★	★★★★½	★★★★½	★★★★½

Duration of Presentation: About 20 minutes

Preshow Entertainment: Explanatory lead-in to feature presentation

Probable Waiting Time: Less than 10 minutes at times suggested

The Making of Me

What It Is: Humorous movie about human conception and birth

Scope & Scale: Minor attraction

Fright Potential: Not frightening in any respect

Bottleneck Rating: 10

When to Go: Early in the morning or after 4:30 p.m.

Author's Rating: Sanitized sex education; ★★★

Appeal by Age Group:

Pre-school	Grade School	Teens	Young Adults	Over 30	Senior Citizens
★½	★★★½	★★½	★★★	★★★	★★★

Duration of Presentation: 14 minutes

Preshow Entertainment: None

Probable Waiting Time: 25 minutes or more, unless you go at suggested times

UNIVERSE OF ENERGY: ELLEN'S ENERGY ADVENTURE

What It Is: Combination ride/theater presentation about energy

Scope & Scale: Major attraction

Fright Potential: Dinosaur segment frightens some preschoolers; visually intense, with some intimidating effects

Bottleneck Rating: 8

When to Go: Before 11:15 a.m. or after 4:30 p.m.

Special Comments: Don't be dismayed by long lines; 580 people enter the pavilion each time the theater turns over

Author's Rating: The most improved attraction at Walt Disney World; ★★★★

Appeal by Age Group:

Pre-school	Grade School	Teens	Young Adults	Over 30	Senior Citizens
★★★	★★★★	★★★½	★★★★	★★★★	★★★★

Duration of Presentation: About 26½ minutes

Preshow Entertainment: 8 minutes

Probable Waiting Time: 20–40 minutes

World Showcase

World Showcase, Epcot's second theme area, is an ongoing World's Fair encircling a picturesque, 40-acre lagoon. The cuisine, culture, history, and architecture of almost a dozen countries are permanently displayed in individual national pavilions spaced along a 1.2-mile promenade. Pavilions replicate familiar landmarks and present representative street scenes from the host countries.

MEXICO PAVILION
El Río del Tiempo

What It Is: Indoor scenic boat ride

Scope & Scale: Minor attraction

Fright Potential: Not frightening in any respect

Bottleneck Rating: 5

When to Go: Before 11 a.m. or after 3 p.m.

Author's Rating: Light and relaxing; ★★

Appeal by Age Group:

Pre-school	Grade School	Teens	Young Adults	Over 30	Senior Citizens
★★★	★★	★½	★★	★★	★★½

Duration of Ride: About 7 minutes

Average Wait in Line per 100 People ahead of You: 4½ minutes

Norway Pavilion

Maelstrom

What It Is: Indoor adventure boat ride

Scope & Scale: Major attraction

Fright Potential: Dark, visually intense in parts. Ride ends with a plunge down a 20-foot flume

Bottleneck Rating: 9

When to Go: Before noon or after 4:30 p.m.

Author's Rating: Too short, but has its moments; ★★★

Appeal by Age Group:

Pre-school	Grade School	Teens	Young Adults	Over 30	Senior Citizens
★★★½	★★★½	★★★	★★★	★★★	★★★

Duration of Ride: 4½ minutes, followed by a 5-minute film with a short wait in between; about 14 minutes for the whole show

Average Wait in Line per 100 People ahead of You: 4 minutes

China Pavilion

Wonders of China

What It Is: Film about the Chinese people and country

Scope & Scale: Major attraction

Fright Potential: Not frightening in any respect

Bottleneck Rating: 5

When to Go: Anytime

Special Comments: Audience stands throughout performance

Author's Rating: Well produced, though film glosses over political unrest and events in Tibet; ★★★

Appeal by Age Group:

Pre-school	Grade School	Teens	Young Adults	Over 30	Senior Citizens
★★	★★½	★★★	★★★½	★★★★	★★★★

Duration of Presentation: About 19 minutes

Preshow Entertainment: None

Probable Waiting Time: 10 minutes

GERMANY PAVILION

The Germany Pavilion does not have attractions. The main focus is the Biergarten, a full-service (priority seating required) restaurant serving German food and beer. Yodeling, folk dancing, and oompah band music are included during mealtimes. New at Germany is a large, elaborate model railroad located just beyond the rest rooms as you walk from Germany toward Italy.

ITALY PAVILION

Once again, there are no attractions in this section. The entrance to Italy is marked by a 105-foot-tall campanile (bell tower) said to mirror the tower in St. Mark's Square in Venice. Left of the campanile is a replica of the 14th-century Doge's Palace.

THE AMERICAN ADVENTURE

What It Is: Patriotic mixed-media and Audio-Animatronic theater presentation on U.S. history

Scope & Scale: Headliner

Fright Potential: Not frightening in any respect

Bottleneck Rating: 6

When to Go: Anytime

Author's Rating: Disney's best historic/patriotic attraction; not to be missed; ★★★★

Appeal by Age Group:

Pre-school	Grade School	Teens	Young Adults	Over 30	Senior Citizens
★★	★★★	★★★	★★★★	★★★★½	★★★★★

Duration of Presentation: About 29 minutes

Preshow Entertainment: Voices of Liberty chorale singing

Probable Waiting Time: 16 minutes

JAPAN PAVILION

The five-story, blue-roofed pagoda, inspired by a seventh-century shrine in Nara, sets this pavilion apart. A hill garden behind it encompasses waterfalls, rocks, flowers, lanterns, paths, and rustic bridges. There are no attractions.

MOROCCO PAVILION

The bustling market, winding streets, lofty minarets, and stuccoed archways re-create the romance and intrigue of Marrakesh and Casablanca. Attention to detail makes Morocco one of the most exciting World Showcase pavilions, but there are no attractions.

FRANCE PAVILION

Impressions de France

What It Is: Film essay on the French people and country

Scope & Scale: Major attraction

Fright Potential: Not frightening in any respect

Bottleneck Rating: 8

When to Go: Before noon and after 4 p.m.

Author's Rating: Exceedingly beautiful film; not to be missed;
   ★★★½

Appeal by Age Group:

Pre-school	Grade School	Teens	Young Adults	Over 30	Senior Citizens
★½	★★½	★★★	★★★★	★★★★	★★★★

Duration of Presentation: About 18 minutes
Preshow Entertainment: None
Probable Waiting Time: 12 minutes (at suggested times)

UNITED KINGDOM PAVILION

A variety of period architecture attempts to capture Britain's city, town, and rural atmospheres. One street alone has a thatched-roof cottage, a four-story timber-and-plaster building, a pre-Georgian plaster building, a formal Palladian exterior of dressed stone, and a city square with a Hyde Park bandstand (whew!). There are no attractions.

MILLENNIUM VILLAGE

Inserted between the United Kingdom and Canada is the Millennium Village, a temporary exhibit created for the 15-month, Walt Disney World Millennium celebration. The Village showcases the culture of several countries, including Sweden and Brazil, not previously represented at Epcot. Other Village exhibits are sponsored by corporations who display their products and technologies. Food and drink are available. There are no attractions.

CANADA PAVILION
O Canada!

What It Is: Film essay on the Canadian people and their country
Scope & Scale: Major attraction
Fright Potential: Not frightening in any respect
Bottleneck Rating: 6
When to Go: Anytime
Special Comments: Audience stands during performance
Author's Rating: Makes you want to catch the first plane to Canada! ★★★½

Appeal by Age Group:

Pre-school	Grade School	Teens	Young Adults	Over 30	Senior Citizens
★★	★★½	★★★	★★★½	★★★★	★★★★

Duration of Presentation: About 18 minutes
Preshow Entertainment: None
Probable Waiting Time: 10 minutes

ILLUMINATIONS

What It Is: Nighttime fireworks and laser show
Scope & Scale: Super headliner
Venue: World Showcase Lagoon
Fright Potential: Not frightening in any respect
When to Go: Stake out viewing position 20–40 minutes
    before showtime
Special Comments: Showtime is listed in the daily entertainment
    schedule on the handout park map. Audience stands during
    performance
Author's Rating: Epcot's most impressive entertainment event;
    ★★★★
Appeal by Age Group:

Pre-school	Grade School	Teens	Young Adults	Over 30	Senior Citizens
★★★	★★★★	★★★★	★★★★	★★★★	★★★★

Duration of Presentation: About 14 minutes

Part Eight

The Animal Kingdom

With its lush flora, winding streams, meandering paths, and exotic setting, the Animal Kingdom is a stunningly beautiful theme park. The landscaping alone conjures images of rain forest, veldt, and even formal garden. Add to this loveliness a population of more than 1,000 animals, replicas of Africa's and Asia's most intriguing architecture, and a diverse array of singularly original attractions, and you have the most unique of all Walt Disney World theme parks. When complete, the Animal Kingdom will feature seven sections or "lands": The Oasis, Safari Village, DinoLand U.S.A., Camp Minnie-Mickey, Africa, Asia, and an as yet unnamed land inspired by mythical beasts.

At the entrance plaza are ticket kiosks fronting the main entrance. To your right before the turnstiles you'll find the kennel and an ATM. Passing through the turnstiles, wheelchair and stroller rentals are to your right. Guest Relations, the park headquarters for information, handout park maps, entertainment schedules, missing persons, and lost and found, is to the left.

The park is arranged somewhat like the Magic Kingdom. The lush, tropical Oasis serves as Main Street, funneling visitors to Safari Village on an island at the center of the park. Safari Village is the park's retail and dining center. From Safari Village, guests can access the respective theme areas: Africa, Camp Minnie-Mickey, Asia, and DinoLand U.S.A.

Safari Village

Safari Village is an island of tropical greenery and whimsical equatorial African architecture, executed in vibrant hues of teal, yellow, red, and blue. Connected to the other lands by bridges, the island is the hub from which guests can access the park's various theme areas. In addition to several wildlife exhibits, there are two attractions at Safari Village.

The Tree of Life/It's Tough to Be a Bug!

What It Is: 3D theater show

Scope & Scale: Major attraction

Fright Potential: Very intense and loud with special effects that startle viewers of all ages and potentially terrify young children

Bottleneck Rating: 10

When to Go: Before 10 a.m. and after 4 p.m.

Special Comments: The theater is inside the tree

Author's Rating: Zany and frenetic; ★★★★

Appeal by Age Group:

Pre-school	Grade School	Teens	Young Adults	Over 30	Senior Citizens
★★½	★★★★★	★★★★★	★★★★	★★★★	★★★★

Duration of Presentation: Approximately 7½ minutes

Probable Waiting Time: 12–30 minutes

Radio Disney River Cruise

What It Is: Boat ride

Scope & Scale: Minor attraction

Fright Potential: Not frightening in any respect

Bottleneck Rating: 10

When to Go: Before 10 a.m. or 1 hour before closing

Author's Rating: Not worth the wait; ★

Appeal by Age Group:

Pre-school	Grade School	Teens	Young Adults	Over 30	Senior Citizens
★★	★	½	½	★	★

Duration of Ride: 17 minutes

Average Wait in Line per 100 People ahead of You: 14 minutes

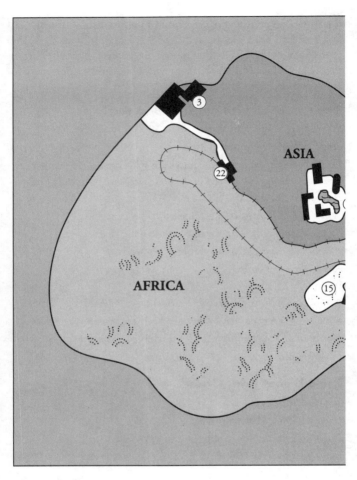

1. The Boneyard
2. Character Greeting Area
3. Conservation Station
4. Countdown to Extinction
5. Cretaceous Trail
6. *Festival of the Lion King*
7. Flights of Wonder
8. Gibbon Pool
9. Guest Relations
10. Harambe Village
11. Kali River Rapids
12. Kilimanjaro Safaris

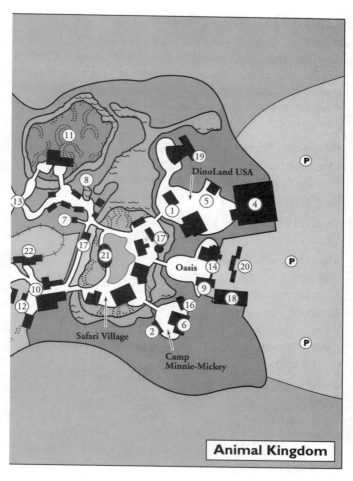

Animal Kingdom

13. Maharaja Jungle Trek
14. Main Entrance
15. Pangani Forest Exploration Trail
16. Pocahontas
17. Radio Disney River Cruise
18. Rainforest Cafe

19. Theater in the Wild
20. Ticket Booths
21. Tree of Life/
    It's Tough to Be Bug!
22. Wildlife Express (Train)

Camp Minnie-Mickey

This land is designed to be the Disney characters' Animal Kingdom headquarters. A small land, Camp Minnie-Mickey is about the size of Mickey's Toontown Fair but has a rustic and woodsy theme like a summer camp. In addition to a character meeting and greeting area, Camp Minnie-Mickey is home to two live stage productions featuring Disney characters.

Character Trails

Characters can be found at the end of each of four "character trails" respectively named Jungle, Forest, Arbor, and Mickey. Each trail has its own private reception area and, of course, its own queue.

Festival of the Lion King

What It Is: Theater-in-the-round stage show

Scope & Scale: Major attraction

Fright Potential: A bit loud, but otherwise not frightening in any respect

Bottleneck Rating: 9

When to Go: Before 11 a.m. or after 4 p.m.

Special Comments: Performance times are listed in the handout park map

Author's Rating: Upbeat and spectacular; ★★★★

Appeal by Age Group:

Pre-school	Grade School	Teens	Young Adults	Over 30	Senior Citizens
★★★★	★★★★½	★★★★	★★★★	★★★★	★★★★

Duration of Presentation: 25 minutes

Preshow Entertainment: None

Probable Waiting Time: 20–35 minutes

Pocahontas and Her Forest Friends at Grandmother Willow's Grove

What It Is: Conservation-themed stage show

Scope & Scale: Major attraction

Fright Potential: Not frightening in any respect

Bottleneck Rating: 7

When to Go: Before 11 a.m. or after 4 p.m.

Special Comments: Performance times are listed in the handout park map

Author's Rating: A little sappy; ★★½

Appeal by Age Group:

Pre-school	Grade School	Teens	Young Adults	Over 30	Senior Citizens
★★★½	★★★½	★★★	★★★½	★★★	★★★

Duration of Presentation: 15 minutes

Preshow Entertainment: None

Probable Waiting Time: 20–30 minutes

Africa

The largest of the Animal Kingdom's lands, guests enter through Harambe, Disney's idealized and immensely sanitized version of a modern rural African town. There is a market (with modern cash registers), and counter-service food is available.

Kilimanjaro Safaris

What It Is: Truck ride through an African wildlife reservation

Scope & Scale: Super headliner

When to Go: Before 9:30 a.m. or in the 2 hours before closing

Fright Potential: A "collapsing" bridge and the proximity of real animals make a few young children anxious

Bottleneck Rating: 10

Author's Rating: Truly exceptional; ★★★★★

Appeal by Age Group:

Pre-school	Grade School	Teens	Young Adults	Over 30	Senior Citizens
★★★★	★★★★★	★★★★½	★★★★½	★★★★½	★★★★★

Duration of Ride: About 20 minutes

Average Wait in Line per 100 People ahead of You: 4 minutes

Pangani Forest Exploration Trail

What it Is: Walk-through zoological exhibit

Scope & Scale: Major attraction

Fright Potential: Not frightening in any respect
Bottleneck Rating: 9
When to Go: Before 9:30 a.m. or in the two hours before closing
Author's Rating: ★★★
Appeal by Age Group:

Pre-school	Grade School	Teens	Young Adults	Over 30	Senior Citizens
★★½	★★★	★★½	★★★	★★★	★★★

Duration of Tour: About 20–25 minutes

Wildlife Express

What It Is: Scenic railroad ride to Conservation Station
Scope & Scale: Major attraction
Fright Potential: Not frightening in any respect
Bottleneck Rating: 7
When to Go: Before 10:30 a.m. or after 4 p.m.
Special Comments: Most guests will take the train after returning
    to Harambe from the Kilimanjaro Safari
Author's Rating: Ho-hum; ★★
Appeal by Age Group:

Pre-school	Grade School	Teens	Young Adults	Over 30	Senior Citizens
★★★	★★★	★½	★★½	★★½	★★½

Duration of Ride: About 5–7 minutes one-way
Average Wait in Line per 100 People ahead of You: 9 minutes

Conservation Station

What It Is: Behind-the-scenes walk-through educational exhibit
Scope & Scale: Minor attraction
Fright Potential: Not frightening in any respect
Bottleneck Rating: 6
When to Go: Before 11 a.m. or after 3 p.m.
Author's Rating: Evolving; ★★★
Probable Waiting Time: None

Appeal by Age Group:

Pre-school	Grade School	Teens	Young Adults	Over 30	Senior Citizens
★★½	★★	★½	★★½	★★½	★★½

Duration of Ride: About 20–40 minutes one-way

Asia

Crossing the Asia Bridge from Safari Village, you enter Asia through the village of Anandapur, a veritable collage of Asian themes inspired by the architecture and ruins of India, Thailand, Indonesia, and Nepal.

Kali River Rapids

What It Is: Whitewater raft ride

Scope & Scale: Headliner

Fright Potential: Potentially frightening and certainly wet for guests of all ages

Bottleneck Rating: 9

When to Go: Before 10 a.m. or after 4:30 p.m.

Special Comments: You are guaranteed to get wet

Author's Rating: ★★★½

Appeal by Age Group:

Pre-school	Grade School	Teens	Young Adults	Over 30	Senior Citizens
★★★★	★★★★	★★★★	★★★½	★★★½	★★★

Duration of Ride: About 5 minutes

Average Wait in Line per 100 People ahead of You: 5 minutes

Maharaja Jungle Trek

What It Is: Walk-through zoological exhibit

Scope & Scale: Headliner

Fright Potential: Some children may balk at the bat exhibit

Bottleneck Rating: 5

When to Go: Anytime

Author's Rating: A standard setter for natural habitat design;
★★★★

Appeal by Age Group:

Pre-school	Grade School	Teens	Young Adults	Over 30	Senior Citizens
★★★	★★★½	★★★	★★★½	★★★★	★★★★

Duration of Tour: About 20–30 minutes

Flights of Wonder at the Caravan Stage

What It Is: Stadium show about birds

Scope & Scale: Major attraction

Fright Potential: Swooping birds startle some younger children

Bottleneck Rating: 6

When to Go: Anytime

Special Comments: Performance times are listed in the handout park map

Author's Rating: Unique; ★★★★

Appeal by Age Group:

Pre-school	Grade School	Teens	Young Adults	Over 30	Senior Citizens
★★★★	★★★★	★★★½	★★★★	★★★★	★★★★

Duration of Presentation: 30 minutes

Preshow Entertainment: None

DinoLand U.S.A.

This most typically Disney of the Animal Kingdom's lands is a cross between an anthropological dig and a quirky roadside attraction. Accessible via the bridge from Safari Village, DinoLand U.S.A. is home to a children's play area, a nature trail, a 1,500-seat amphitheater, a couple of natural history exhibits, and Countdown to Extinction, one of the Animal Kingdom's two thrill rides.

Countdown to Extinction

What It Is: Motion-simulator dark ride

Scope & Scale: Super headliner

Fright Potential: High-tech thrill ride rattles riders of all ages

Bottleneck Rating: 8

When to Go: Before 10 a.m. or in the hour before closing

Special Comments: Children must be 46" tall to ride; switching off provided

Author's Rating: Really improved; ★★★★½

Appeal by Age Group:

Pre-school	Grade School	Teens	Young Adults	Over 30	Senior Citizens
†	★★★★½	★★★★½	★★★★½	★★★★½	★★★½

† Sample size too small for an accurate rating

Duration of Ride: 3 ⅓ minutes

Average Wait in Line per 100 People ahead of You: 3 minutes

Theater in the Wild

What It Is: Open-air venue for live stage shows

Scope & Scale: Major attraction

Fright Potential: Not frightening in any respect

Bottleneck Rating: 6

When to Go: Anytime

Special Comments: Performance times are listed in the handout park map

Author's Rating: ★★★★

Appeal by Age Group:

Pre-school	Grade School	Teens	Young Adults	Over 30	Senior Citizens
★★★★	★★★★	★★★★	★★★★	★★★★	★★★★

Duration of Presentation: 25–35 minutes

Preshow Entertainment: None

Probable Waiting Time: 20–30 minutes

The Boneyard

What It Is: Elaborate playground

Scope & Scale: Diversion

Fright Potential: Not frightening in any respect

Bottleneck Rating: 5

When to Go: Anytime

Author's Rating: Stimulating fun for children; ★★★½

Appeal by Age Group:

Pre-school	Grade School	Teens	Young Adults	Over 30	Senior Citizens
★★★★½	★★★★½	†	†	†	†

† Sample sizes too small for accurate ratings

Duration of Visit: Varies

Waiting Time: None

Cretaceous Trail

What It Is: Walk-through floral exhibit

Scope & Scale: Diversion

Fright Potential: Not frightening in any respect

Bottleneck Rating: 3

When to Go: Anytime

Author's Rating: Stretches a point to be called an "attraction"; ★½

Appeal by Age Group:

Pre-school	Grade School	Teens	Young Adults	Over 30	Senior Citizens
★½	★★	★★	★½	★★	★★

Duration of Visit: Varies

Waiting Time: None

Part Nine

The Disney-MGM Studios

About half of the Disney-MGM Studios is set up as a theme park. The other half, off-limits except by guided tour, is a working motion picture and television studio. Though modest in size, the open-access areas of the Studios are confusingly arranged (a product of the park's hurried expansion in the early '90s). As at the Magic Kingdom, you enter the park and pass down a main street, only this time it's Hollywood Boulevard of the 1920s and '30s. Because there are no "lands" as in the other parks, the easiest way to navigate is by landmarks and attractions using the park map.

Guest Relations, on your left as you enter, serves as the park headquarters and information center, similar to City Hall in the Magic Kingdom and Guest Relations at Epcot and the Animal Kingdom. Go there for a schedule of live performances, lost persons, Package Pick-up, lost and found (on the right side of the entrance), general information, or in an emergency. If you haven't received a map of the Studios, get one here. To the right of the entrance are locker, stroller, and wheelchair rentals.

Disney-MGM Studios Attractions

The Twilight Zone Tower of Terror

What It Is: Sci-fi-theme indoor thrill ride

Scope & Scale: Super headliner

Fright Potential: Visually intimidating to young children; contains intense and realistic special effects. The plummeting elevator at the ride's end frightens many adults. Switching off is provided

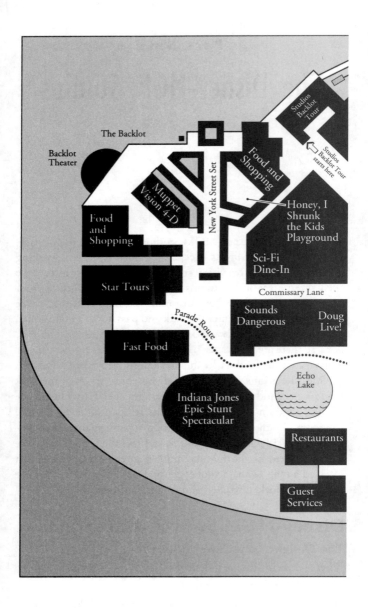

The Backlot

Backlot Theater

Food and Shopping

Muppet Vision 4-D

New York Street Set

Food and Shopping

Studios Backlot Tour

Studios Backlot Tour starts here

Honey, I Shrunk the Kids Playground

Sci-Fi Dine-In

Commissary Lane

Star Tours

Parade Route

Sounds Dangerous

Doug Live!

Fast Food

Echo Lake

Indiana Jones Epic Stunt Spectacular

Restaurants

Guest Services

194

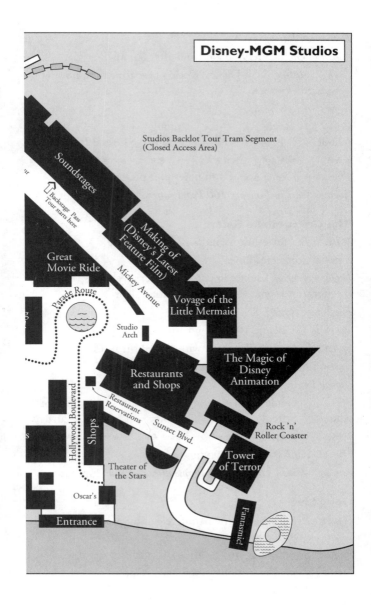

Disney-MGM Studios

Studios Backlot Tour Tram Segment
(Closed Access Area)

Soundstages

Backstage Pass
Tour starts here

Making of
(Disney's Latest
Feature Film)

Great
Movie Ride

Mickey Avenue

Voyage of the
Little Mermaid

Parade Route

Studio
Arch

The Magic of
Disney
Animation

Restaurants
and Shops

Hollywood Boulevard

Restaurant
Reservations

Sunset Blvd.

Rock 'n'
Roller Coaster

Shops

Tower
of Terror

Theater of
the Stars

Oscar's

Entrance

Fantasmic!

Bottleneck Rating: 10

When to Go: Before 9:30 a.m. and after 6 p.m.

Author's Rating: Walt Disney World's best attraction; not to be missed; ★★★★★

Appeal by Age Group:

Pre-school	Grade School	Teens	Young Adults	Over 30	Senior Citizens
★★★	★★★★★	★★★★★	★★★★★	★★★★★	★★★★½

Duration of Ride: About 4 minutes plus preshow

Average Wait in Line per 100 People ahead of You: 4 minutes

The Great Movie Ride

What It Is: Movie-history indoor adventure ride

Scope & Scale: Headliner

Fright Potential: Intense in parts, with very realistic special effects and some visually intimidating sights

Bottleneck Rating: 8

When to Go: Before 10 a.m. and after 5 p.m.

Special Comments: Elaborate, with several surprises

Author's Rating: Unique; ★★★½

Appeal by Age Group:

Pre-school	Grade School	Teens	Young Adults	Over 30	Senior Citizens
★★½	★★★½	★★★½	★★★★	★★★★	★★★★

Duration of Ride: About 19 minutes

Average Wait in Line per 100 People ahead of You: 2 minutes

Doug Live!

What It Is: Audience-participation television production based on Disney Doug cartoon

Scope & Scale: Major attraction

Fright Potential: Not frightening in any respect

Bottleneck Rating: 4

When to Go: After 10 a.m.

Author's Rating: Pure smaltz; ★★½

Appeal by Age Group:

Pre-school	Grade School	Teens	Young Adults	Over 30	Senior Citizens
★★★½	★★★½	★★	★★★	★★½	★★½

Duration of Presentation: 30 minutes

Preshow Entertainment: Participants selected from guests waiting in the preshow area

Probable Waiting Time: 10–20 minutes

Star Tours

What It Is: Indoor space flight–simulation ride

Scope & Scale: Headliner

Fright Potential: Extremely intense visually for all ages; the ride is one of Disney's wildest. Likely to cause motion sickness. Switching off is provided

Bottleneck Rating: 8

When to Go: First hour and a half the park is open

Special Comments: Expectant mothers or anyone prone to motion sickness are advised against riding. The ride is too intense for many children younger than age 8

Author's Rating: Not to be missed; ★★★★

Appeal by Age Group:

Pre-school	Grade School	Teens	Young Adults	Over 30	Senior Citizens
★★★★	★★★★	★★★★	★★★★	★★★★	★★★★

Duration of Ride: About 7 minutes

Average Wait in Line per 100 People ahead of You: 5 minutes

Rock 'n' Roller Coaster

What It Is: Disney's wildest roller coaster

Scope & Scale: Headliner

Fright Potential: Extremely intense for all ages; the ride is one of Disney's wildest. Switching off is provided

Bottleneck Rating: 9

When to Go: First hour the park is open

Special Comments: Expectant mothers or anyone prone to
    motion sickness are advised against riding. The ride is too
    intense for many children younger than age 8

Author's Rating: Not to be missed; ★★★★

Appeal by Age Group:

Pre-school	Grade School	Teens	Young Adults	Over 30	Senior Citizens
★★★	★★★★½	★★★★½	★★★★½	★★★★½	★½

Duration of Ride: About 3 minutes

Average Wait in Line per 100 People ahead of You: 7 minutes

Sounds Dangerous

What It Is: Show demonstrating sound effects

Scope & Scale: Minor attraction

Fright Potential: Sounds in darkened theater frighten some
    preschoolers.

Bottleneck Rating: 6

When to Go: Before 11 a.m. or after 5 p.m.

Author's Rating: Funny and informative; ★★★

Appeal by Age Group:

Pre-school	Grade School	Teens	Young Adults	Over 30	Senior Citizens
★★½	★★★½	★★★	★★★	★★★	★★★

Duration of Presentation: 12 minutes

Preshow Entertainment: Video introduction to sound effects

Probable Waiting Time: 15–30 minutes

Indiana Jones Epic Stunt Spectacular

What It Is: Movie-stunt demonstration and action show

Scope & Scale: Headliner

Fright Potential: An intense show with powerful special effects,
    including explosions. Presented in an educational context
    that young children generally handle well

Bottleneck Rating: 8

When to Go: First three morning shows or last evening show

Special Comments: Performance times posted on a sign at the entrance to the theater

Author's Rating: Done on a grand scale; ★★★★

Appeal by Age Group:

Pre-school	Grade School	Teens	Young Adults	Over 30	Senior Citizens
★★★	★★★★	★★★★	★★★★	★★★★	★★★★

Duration of Presentation: 30 minutes

Preshow Entertainment: Selection of "extras" from audience

Theater of the Stars

What It Is: Live, Hollywood-style musical, usually featuring Disney characters; performed in an open-air theater

Scope & Scale: Major attraction

Fright Potential: Not frightening in any respect

Bottleneck Rating: 5

When to Go: In the evening

Special Comments: Performances are listed in the daily entertainment schedule

Author's Rating: Excellent; ★★★★

Appeal by Age Group:

Pre-school	Grade School	Teens	Young Adults	Over 30	Senior Citizens
★★★★	★★★★	★★★	★★★★	★★★★	★★★★

Duration of Presentation: 25 minutes

Preshow Entertainment: None

Probable Waiting Time: 20–30 minutes

Fantasmic!

What It Is: Mixed-media nighttime spectacular

Scope & Scale: Super headliner

Fright Potential: Loud and intense with fireworks, but most young children like it

Bottleneck Rating: 9

When to Go: Only staged in the evening

Special Comments: Disney's best nighttime event
Author's Rating: Not to be missed; ★★★★★
Appeal by Age Group:

Pre-school	Grade School	Teens	Young Adults	Over 30	Senior Citizens
★★★★	★★★★★	★★★★½	★★★★½	★★★★½	★★★★½

Duration of Presentation: 25 minutes
Probable Waiting Time: 60 minutes if you want a seat; 30 minutes for standing room

Voyage of the Little Mermaid

What It Is: Musical stage show featuring characters from the Disney movie *The Little Mermaid*
Scope & Scale: Major attraction
Fright Potential: Not frightening in any respect
Bottleneck Rating: 10
When to Go: Before 9:45 a.m. or just before closing
Author's Rating: Romantic, lovable, and humorous in the best Disney tradition; not to be missed; ★★★★
Appeal by Age Group:

Pre-school	Grade School	Teens	Young Adults	Over 30	Senior Citizens
★★★★	★★★★	★★★½	★★★★	★★★★	★★★★

Duration of Presentation: 15 minutes
Preshow Entertainment: Taped ramblings about the decor in the preshow holding area
Probable Waiting Time: Before 9:30 a.m., 10–30 minutes; after 9:30 a.m., 35–70 minutes

The Making of (Disney's Latest Feature Film)

What It Is: Documentary about the making of Disney's latest feature film
Scope & Scale: Minor attraction
Fright Potential: Not frightening in any respect

Bottleneck Rating: 4
When to Go: Anytime
Author's Rating: Disney infomercial; ★★★
Appeal by Age Group:

Pre-school	Grade School	Teens	Young Adults	Over 30	Senior Citizens
★★	★★★	★★★½	★★★½	★★★½	★★★½

Duration of Presentation: 17 minutes
Preshow Entertainment: Tour of postproduction facilities
Probable Waiting Time: 20 minutes

Jim Henson's MuppetVision 4D

What It Is: 4D movie starring the Muppets
Scope & Scale: Major attraction
Fright Potential: Intense and loud, but not frightening
Bottleneck Rating: 8
When to Go: Before 11 a.m. and after 4 p.m.
Author's Rating: Uproarious; not to be missed; ★★★★½
Appeal by Age Group:

Pre-school	Grade School	Teens	Young Adults	Over 30	Senior Citizens
★★★★½	★★★★½	★★★★½	★★★★½	★★★★½	★★★★½

Duration of Presentation: 17 minutes
Preshow Entertainment: Muppets on television
Probable Waiting Time: 12 minutes

Honey, I Shrunk the Kids Movie Set Adventure

What It Is: Small but elaborate playground
Scope & Scale: Diversion
Fright Potential: Everything is oversized, but nothing is scary
Bottleneck Rating: 7
When to Go: Before 10 a.m. or after dark
Author's Rating: Great for young children, optional for adults;
　　★★½

Appeal by Age Group:

Pre-school	Grade School	Teens	Young Adults	Over 30	Senior Citizens
★★★★½	★★★½	★★	★★½	★★★	★★½

Duration of Presentation: Varies

Average Wait in Line per 100 People ahead of You: 20 minutes

New York Street Backlot

What It Is: Walk-through backlot movie set

Scope & Scale: Diversion

Fright Potential: Not frightening in any respect

Bottleneck Rating: 1

When to Go: Anytime

Author's Rating: Interesting, with great detail; ★★★

Appeal by Age Group:

Pre-school	Grade School	Teens	Young Adults	Over 30	Senior Citizens
★½	★★★	★★★	★★★	★★★	★★★

Duration of Presentation: Varies

Average Wait in Line per 100 People ahead of You: No waiting

Backlot Theater

What It Is: Live, Hollywood-style musical, usually based on a Disney film, and performed in an open-air theater

Scope & Scale: Major attraction

Fright Potential: Not frightening in any respect

Bottleneck Rating: 7

When to Go: First show in the morning, or any show in the evening

Special Comments: Performance times are listed in the daily entertainment schedule

Author's Rating: Excellent; ★★★★

Appeal by Age Group:

Pre-school	Grade School	Teens	Young Adults	Over 30	Senior Citizens
★★★	★★★½	★★★	★★★★	★★★★	★★★★

Duration of Presentation: 25–35 minutes
Preshow Entertainment: None
Probable Waiting Time: 20–30 minutes

The Magic of Disney Animation

What It Is: Walking tour of the Disney Animation Studio
Scope & Scale: Major attraction
Fright Potential: Not frightening in any respect
Bottleneck Rating: 7
When to Go: Before 11 a.m. and after 5 p.m.
Author's Rating: A masterpiece; not to be missed; ★★★★
Appeal by Age Group:

Pre-school	Grade School	Teens	Young Adults	Over 30	Senior Citizens
★★★	★★★	★★★	★★★★	★★★★	★★★★

Duration of Presentation: 36 minutes
Average Wait in Line per 100 People ahead of You: 7 minutes

Disney-MGM Studios Backlot Tour

What It Is: Combination tram and walking tour of modern film and video production
Scope & Scale: Headliner
Fright Potential: Sedate and nonintimidating except for "Catastrophe Canyon," where an earthquake and flash flood are simulated. Prepare younger children for this part of the tour
Bottleneck Rating: 6
When to Go: Anytime
Author's Rating: Educational and fun; not to be missed; ★★★★
Appeal by Age Group:

Pre-school	Grade School	Teens	Young Adults	Over 30	Senior Citizens
★★★	★★★★	★★★★	★★★★	★★★★	★★★★

Duration of Presentation: About 25 minutes
Special Comments: Can be combined with soundstage tour described below

Preshow Entertainment: A video before the special effects segment and another video in the tram boarding area

Average Wait in Line per 100 People ahead of You: 2 minutes

Backstage Pass

What It Is: Walking tour of modern film and video production soundstages

Scope & Scale: Minor attraction

Fright Potential: Not frightening in any respect

Bottleneck Rating: 6

When to Go: Anytime

Author's Rating: Latest version not the best, but still informative; ★★★

Appeal by Age Group:

Pre-school	Grade School	Teens	Young Adults	Over 30	Senior Citizens
★½	★★	★★	★★★	★★★	★★★

Duration of Presentation: About 25 minutes

Special Comments: Can be combined with Disney-MGM Studios Backlot Tour described above

Probable Waiting Time: 10 minutes

Live Entertainment

In addition to *Fantasmic!* (described above) the Studios offer an afternoon parade.

Part Ten

The Rest of the World

The Water Theme Parks

Walt Disney World has three swimming theme parks. River Country is the oldest and smallest park. Typhoon Lagoon, about five years old, is the most diverse Disney splash pad, while three-year-old Blizzard Beach takes the prize for the most slides and most bizarre theme (a ski resort in meltdown).

Although children love all three parks, River Country doesn't begin to measure up to the two newer parks in terms of size, slides, diversity, or, for that matter, crowds. Simply put, if you plan only one or two days at the swimming parks, River Country is the least interesting for all kids and for most adults. Blizzard Beach has the best slides, but Typhoon Lagoon has a surf pool where you can body surf. All of the parks have excellent and elaborate themed areas for toddlers and preschoolers.

At all Disney water parks, the following rules and prices apply: One cooler per family or group is allowed, but no glass and no alcoholic beverages; towels $1, small locker $3, large locker $5 ($2 deposit required for lockers), life jacket $25 refundable deposit.

The best way to avoid standing in lines is to visit the water parks when they're less crowded. Because the parks are popular among locals, weekends can be tough. We recommend going on a Monday or Tuesday, when locals will be at work or school and most other tourists will be visiting the Magic Kingdom, Epcot, the Animal Kingdom, or Disney-MGM Studios. Fridays are good because people traveling by car often use this day to start home. Sunday morning also has lighter crowds. During summer and holiday periods, Typhoon Lagoon and Blizzard Beach fill to capacity and close their gates before 11 a.m.

If you are going to Blizzard Beach or Typhoon Lagoon, get up early, have breakfast, and arrive at the park 40 minutes before opening. If you have a car, drive instead of taking a Disney bus. If you're going to River Country, you don't have to get there so early.

Wear your bathing suit under shorts and a T-shirt so you don't need to use lockers or dressing rooms. Wear shoes. Paths are relatively easy on bare feet, but there's a lot of ground to cover. If you or your children have tender feet, wear your shoes as you move around the park, removing them when you raft, slide, or go into the water. Shops in the parks sell sandals, "Reef Runners," and other protective footwear that can be worn in and out of the water.

You will need a towel, suntan lotion or sun block, and money. Wallets and purses get in the way, so lock them in your car's trunk or leave them at your hotel. Carry enough money for the day and your Disney resort ID (if you have one) in a plastic bag or Tupperware container. Though nowhere is completely safe, we felt very comfortable hiding our plastic money bags in our cooler. Nobody disturbed our stuff, and our cash was much easier to reach than if we'd stashed it in a locker across the park. If you're carrying a wad or you worry about money anyway, rent the locker.

Personal swim gear (fins, masks, rafts, and so on) aren't allowed. Everything you need is either provided or available to rent. If you forget your towel, you can rent one (cheap!). If you forget your swimsuit or lotion, they're available for sale. Personal flotation devices (life jackets) are available free of charge, but you must leave a credit card number or a driver's license as a deposit.

Establish your base for the day. There are many beautiful sunning and lounging spots scattered throughout all Disney swimming parks. Arrive early, and you can almost have your pick. The breeze is best along the beaches of the lagoon at Blizzard Beach and the surf pool at Typhoon Lagoon. At River Country, pick a spot that fronts Bay Lake. At Typhoon Lagoon, if there are children younger than age six in your party, choose an area to the left of Mount Mayday (ship on top) near the children's swimming area.

Though Typhoon Lagoon and Blizzard Beach are huge parks with many slides, armies of guests overwhelm them almost daily. If your main reason for going is the slides and you hate long lines, try to be among the first guests to enter the park. Go directly to the slides and ride as many times as you can before the park fills. When lines for the slides become intolerable, head for the surf or wave pool or the tube-floating streams.

The water parks are large and require almost as much walking as one of the major theme parks. Add to this wave surfing, swimming, and climbing to reach the slides, and you'll definitely be pooped by day's end. Consider something low-key for the evening.

It's as easy to lose a child or become separated from your party at one of the water parks as it is at a major theme park. On arrival, pick a very specific place to meet in the event you are separated. If you split up on purpose, establish times for checking in. Lost-children stations at the water parks are so out of the way that neither you nor your lost child will find them without help from a Disney employee. Explain to your children how to recognize a Disney employee (by their distinctive name tags) and how to ask for help.

Downtown Disney

Downtown Disney comprises the Disney Village Marketplace, Pleasure Island, and Disney's West Side. All three are shopping, dining, and entertainment complexes. Admission is charged at Pleasure Island in the evening, and at the entertainment venues on Disney's West Side. Otherwise, you can roam, shop, and dine without paying any sort of entrance fee.

Pleasure Island   Pleasure Island offers eight nightclubs with entertainment ranging from comedy to jazz to various genres of rock. Once you have paid your admission and passed through the turnstiles, you can hop from club to club without any additional entrance fee or cover charge. You can buy drinks at the various clubs, or if you prefer, just soak up the entertainment without buying a thing. From a family perspective, what's different about Pleasure Island is that kids in the company of their parents are welcome in all but two of the clubs. For most children, going to a nightclub and dancing to a live band with mom and dad is very cool, an experience they won't soon forget; nor, as this mom from Somerset, Kentucky, reports, will their parents:

> *I danced with my 10-year-old at the Beach Club. First thing I know he's down on his back, spinning on his head, and doing all these amazing break dancing moves! Who knew? I wish we had a video camera.*

Under 21s at Pleasure Island are given a wrist band that identifies them as underage for alcohol consumption, so if you want to turn your teens loose during the evening, you won't have to worry about them boozing it up. Pleasure Island really cranks up around 9 or 10 p.m.

DisneyQuest   If your children are age 11 and older, Disney-Quest on Disney's West Side is a special treat you might want to consider. DisneyQuest is Disney's pioneering prototype of a theme park in a box, or more literally, in a modest five-story building.

Opened in the summer of 1998, DisneyQuest contains all the elements of the larger Disney theme parks. There is an entrance area that facilitates your transition into the park environment and leads to the gateways of four distinct themed lands, referred to here as zones. As at other Disney parks, everything is included in the price of your admission.

It takes about two to three hours to experience DisneyQuest, once you get in. Disney limits the number of guests admitted to ensure that queues are manageable and that guests have a positive experience. Weekdays before 4 p.m. are least crowded.

DisneyQuest is aimed at a youthful audience, say 8 to 35 years of age, though younger and older patrons will enjoy much of what it offers. The feel is dynamic, bustling, and noisy. Those who haunt the electronic games arcades at shopping malls will feel most at home at DisneyQuest.

From the turnstile you enter the Departure Lobby and a "Cyberlator," a sort of "transitional attraction" (read elevator) hosted by the genie from *Aladdin,* that delivers you to an entrance plaza called Ventureport. From here you can enter the four zones. Like in the larger parks, each zone is distinctively themed. Some zones cover more than one floor, so, looking around, you can see things going on both above and below you. The four zones, in no particular order, are Explore Zone, Score Zone, Create Zone, and Replay Zone. In addition to the zones, DisneyQuest offers two restaurants and the inevitable gift shop.

Each zone offers several attractions, most based on technologies like simulators that work well in confined spaces. The Explore Zone is representative. You enter through a re-creation of the tiger's-head cave from *Aladdin.* The headline attraction in Explore Zone is the Virtual Jungle Cruise, where you paddle a six-person raft. The raft is a motion simulator perched on top of blue air bags that replicate the motion of water. Responding to the film of the river projected before you, you can choose several routes through the rapids. The motion simulator responds to sensors on your paddle, so the ride you experience simulates the course you choose. As if navigating the river isn't enough, man-eating dinosaurs and a cataclysmic comet are tossed in for good measure. Another Explore Zone attraction, Aladdin's Magic Carpet Ride, has you seated on a motorcycle-shaped simulator. Here you are fitted with a head-mounted virtual reality display. Leaning left and right on your faux motorcycle allows you to navigate your magic carpet through the streets of Agraba.

Some DisneyQuest attractions tap your imagination. In the Create Zone, for example, you can use a computer to design your own roller coaster, including 360° loops, and then take a virtual reality–motion simulator ride on your creation. Also in the Create Zone is Sid's Make-a-Toy, where you can design a toy and receive the parts to actually construct it at home. Other creative attractions include virtual beauty salon makeovers and painting on an electronic canvas.

Like all things Disney, admission to DisneyQuest is not cheap. But especially for teens and technology junkies, it's an eye-opening experience and a fun time.

The Best of the Rest

Unless you're a gambler or a nudist, you'll probably find your favorite activity offered at Walt Disney World. You can fish, canoe, hike, bike, boat, play tennis and golf, ride horses, work out, take cooking lessons, even drive a real race car or watch the Atlanta Braves' spring training. It's all there, along with myriad worthy out-of-the-World diversions such as Sea World, Busch Gardens, and the Universal parks. You may experience bankruptcy, but probably not boredom. And though we cover all of the above in our *Unofficial Guide* family of books on Walt Disney World and central Florida, it's way too much to cram into this modest guide.

One recommendation we can make, however, is that you visit the Wilderness Lodge Resort. Your kids will go nuts, and so will you. While you're there, have a family-style meal at the children-friendly Whispering Canyon restaurant and rent bikes for a ride on the paved paths of adjacent Fort Wilderness campground. The outing will be a great change of pace. The only downside is that your kids might not want to go back to their own hotel.

Index